Young Children Learning

Exploration
and Language

Alice Yardley

Rubicon Publishing

1493

Cover design: Holly Fisher and Associates
Cover photo: Gilles Benoit/Hot Shots

The publishers gratefully acknowledge Wendy Auger
for her contribution to the publication of
the Young Children Learning Series

ISBN: 0-921156-01-4

Canadian Cataloguing in Publication Data

Yardley, Alice.
  Exploration and language

(Young children learning series)
Bibliography: p. 111
Includes index.
ISBN 0-921156-01-4. - ISBN 0-921156-06-5 (set)

1. Children - Language. I. Title. II. Series:
Yardley, Alice. Young children learning series.

LB1139.L3Y37 1987   372.6   C87-095216-1

Printed in Canada by Del/Charters Litho Inc.
1 2 3 4 5   92 91 90 89 88

Contents

Author's Note

This book is a part of the Young Children Learning series in which issues affecting the organization and work of schools for young children are considered. Each book covers a range of topics connected with a particular aspect of the child's life in school. While the ideas expressed in *Reaching Out* provide the foundation on which the other books are based, each book is complete in itself. Some aspects of the work intentionally overlap, and where this occurs the material is considered from different standpoints.

In recent years educators have advanced their skills of observing children. They learn about children from children themselves and modern educational practice aims to provide learning opportunities for young children which are closely related to observed developmental needs. Practice based on observation gives rise to theory and theoretical aims remain flexible instead of dominating practice.

Equally significant has been the deepening trend towards involving parents in all matters affecting the care and education of their children. Parents have taken up this challenge in a number of ways. In the U.K., for example, the mid '60s saw the establishment of the Preschool Playgroups Association Movement. This self-help community service now exists in all parts of the country helping parents to understand and provide for the needs of their young children The under fives in particular benefit enormously from well-planned play facilities and the Playgroups are organized and run by parents who have attended courses which prepare them for these responsibilities. The outcome is well-informed parents who understand the purposes of education. Similar movements flourish in many countries. Likewise the need for parents and teachers to work together has gained universal recognition.

These books then are written for parents as much as for teachers in training, for practising teachers and for all members of the community who are interested in the education of young children. The text is supported throughout by factual examples from situations in the home or the classroom, or from wherever children may be found in the community. The aim generally is to express educational theory in terms of the work of teachers and children.

Many of the views held by educators today are the outcome of personal experience. Not all of them have been tested and proved by research. Indeed, some findings may appear so obviously true to those who know children well that to provide support for them by clinical methods would seem unnecessary. Parents and practising teachers have many things to tell the psychologist. Much of what they do is rooted in their intuitive understanding of children and their behaviour. They may not always be able to explain why they apply certain methods, or how they come by their beliefs. This does not invalidate their work and beliefs, and the psychologist would be the first to admit that there are few definite answers to many questions associated with the upbringing and education of young children.

Throughout I have recorded as simply as possible what I believe to be true about children and I quote extensively from personal experience and from the experience of parents, teachers and children I know well. My first intention is to capture the joy shared by adults and children who are privileged to work alongside one another in the schools of today.

Many people have helped me to collect and prepare my material and I should like to acknowledge my indebtedness to them. Some gave me help in special ways. José Moss provided material for the chapter on slow-learning and gifted children in *Reaching Out.* Margaret Smith outlined the approach to understanding history and Allen Young to understanding geography in *Discovering the Physical World.* Other specialist colleagues helped to check relevant parts of the text. Douglas Kaye assisted with mathematics and John Tollyfield with science in *Discovering The Physical World,* and Robin Protheroe with divinity and Malcolm Anderton with music in *Senses and Sensitivity.*

At all points in the series I am indebted to two very special people. First to my former colleague Allen Young for his advice on learning theory and research and for his infinite patience in checking the original text. Second to my Canadian colleague Wendy Auger for the very skilful and perceptive way in which she has revised the text for publication in Canada.

Finally, I must record my gratitude to all those children, their parents and their teachers who for many years have shared their experiences so generously with me.

Alice Yardley
1987

Introduction

Over the last few years, there has been a concentrated interest in the whole area of early childhood education. As more and more teachers look for guidance in meeting the needs of children in their care, one name comes to the fore. Alice Yardley, a noted educator in England, has long been recognized for her leadership in the field of early childhood in Britain and now Canadians will be the recipients of her ideas through this series of books on how children grow and learn. Already Alice is well-known to many teachers in Canada as she has spent part of each year sharing her wealth of knowledge on lecture tours. Her speaking engagements have taken her from the Maritimes to British Columbia and for the past three years, she has taught Canadian teachers on courses in England.

The message that Alice shares, consistently, is that we must look to children if we are to learn what their needs are and to trust our instincts in dealing with children. She challenges us to be more open and flexible in our interactions and to modify our expectations in responding to their needs. The influence that children have had on Alice is evident throughout the books in this series. Her references to children illustrate insights that she has developed into the teaching/learning process and show amply how Alice has lived a child-centred philosophy throughout her professional life.

This series of books will serve as an on-going resource for teachers who are already familiar with Alice's special views on the young and will be equally useful for those parents and teachers who are meeting her for the first time. I know that you will find her writing style very readable and practical. She has the ability to encapsulate the essence of what it is to be a child in just a few words or sentences. I know that you will be as inspired as I have been by the work of Alice Yardley.

Wendy Auger
York University, 1987

1

Experience into words

Perhaps the most significant event in a child's life occurs at about the age of twelve months. He utters his first word intentionally and with meaning. His parents greet the event with great delight, for they know that their child is acquiring his most important means of understanding. From now on words will provide him with a highly effective medium of communication, and through using words he will become increasingly conscious of his surroundings and of himself.

People are social beings and need to communicate. They communicate mostly by using language, and words are the most important units of language. Only human beings know how to use words. Words give them power over their environment and enable them to manipulate other people.

In our society the articulate person leads. She influences the minds of others, and the highly articulate person inspires reverence and sometimes fear in her colleagues. Her very competence may render others inarticulate and make them feel inadequate. Our civilization is shaped and held together by words. If words were taken away, the world as we know it would disintegrate. Skill in the acquisition and use of words is the prime aim of education in the schools.

On entering school at the age of five, Celia appeared to be perfectly normal. However, she made no attempt to take part in what was happening. She made no response when spoken to. She just sat, her grey eyes giving nothing away as they followed the activities of the children round her. After two weeks the teacher became worried by her refusal to speak. She spoke to Celia's seven-year-old sister, June, to confirm that Celia could, in fact, speak. "Oh, she knows," June assured the teacher. "She's always been shy."

Eventually the teacher learned that Celia was the youngest of a family of five girls whose ages ranged from Celia, aged five, to Patsy aged eighteen. Celia, with four little "mothers" besides her adult mother, found most of her needs

1

anticipated and satisfied without being forced to express them. When she entered school she lacked the normal means of learning. It was difficult to assess her understanding and impossible to estimate her mental powers. It took years at school to encourage her to communicate adequately with others. Throughout her school career her handicap was enormous. Her ability to cope with the literate world she inherited was severely impaired.

When we listen to the skilled oratory of a politician, when we are moved by the words of a play, when we hear the incessant chatter of people round us, it is difficult to realize that so many words – and ways of using them – originated in the baby's first simple sounds. The baby's first cry becomes a means of communicating his needs to someone who responds. From his first breath the baby utters simple sounds, and the long and complicated process of learning about words and growing into the use of them has begun. The drive which forces the child to accomplish speech is founded in his need to survive.

If the child is to learn how to live in the world, she must make sense of her surroundings. Her natural curiosity moves her to explore. For the first year or so she must do this without words. She cannot depend on being told what to do, she must rely on her own resources. It is through her sensory experiences and the emotions associated with them that she collects and retains information. In other parts of this series (*Reaching Out*, Chapter 3, and *Discovering the Physical World*) we consider in some detail the way in which a child gains her knowledge of the world. Here we shall concern ourselves primarily with the way in which she organizes this information.

As the number of his experiences increases, the baby becomes aware that groups of experiences have something in common. He comes to appreciate connections between this and that and he learns to discriminate between them. Perceiving differences helps him to perceive likenesses. Eventually the essence of what is similar emerges in the form of an idea and at a later stage the adult gives him a word to which he recognizes his idea can be attached. He will continue to associate further similar experiences and the word idea, and so the map of his mind begins to take shape.

Meaning at this stage is embodied in sensory and emotional experience, and the ultimate quality of his thought as an adult is founded on such sensory comprehension. Meaning leads to understanding and these together provide the foundation of the child's intellectual development. Examination of a few of the child's elementary ideas will illustrate this point and show how the words a child uses with meaning represent his understanding of his experiences.

Amongst the baby's basic speech patterns can be heard the "ma-ma", "da-da" sounds, and babies in every country utter these sounds, irrespective of the mother tongue they will later learn. From her first days Wendy's parents talked to her. Sometimes her mother would sing to her and clap her little hands together, using such words as, "Clap hands, clap hands till Daddy comes home". When only a few months old Wendy would rock and croon when she heard her mother singing. When she was uncomfortable or hungry, she would murmur "mum-mum" to herself and this usually meant that she was miserable. At four months old she would utter "ma-ma" or "da-da" quite clearly without associating the sounds with a specific person, object or situation. A few weeks later she would sometimes utter these sounds with pleasure, as though she enjoyed making the sound and hearing herself make it.

By the time she was six months old she would call "ma-ma", "da-da" when she was wet or unhappy. When Mother had attended to her and spoken words of comfort, Wendy would repeat the "ma-ma" sound, as though in gratitude. She was nearly seven months old when she began to associate "da-da" with her father and utter the sound as an intelligible word when he attended to her.

Meanwhile her mother helped her to associate the "ma-ma" sound with herself by talking to her: "Come to ma-ma"! "Ma-ma can hear you". By about seven and a half months Wendy was using the "ma-ma" sound in response to her mother.

Wendy was now well aware of her own utterances. They emerged from her as part of her physical state and she associated both sensory and emotional feeling with them. The soft warmth and comfort of her mother's body, the distress she felt when hungry and the satisfaction of having her hunger appeased, the soothing assurance of her mother's voice were all part of her use and recognition of the "ma-ma" sound. The "da-da" sound she associated with more exciting, vigorous experiences, particularly with clapping and jogging up and down.

In later life the word "mother" or "father" would represent all these early experiences she associated with it, together with experiences she acquired during childhood. In adult life the word "mother" or father" can represent warmth, comfort, satisfaction and frustration. For less fortunate people, it can represent neglect, harshness and even fear. The meaning an individual associates with a word depends on his unique experiences, and meaning varies widely between people.

In a similar way, a number of words are grafted on to basic speech patterns, but the adult gives the child many words which are not directly linked with these basic forms. Some of these will be considered in Chapter 3.

When the child begins to name things, he has begun to impose order on his environment. The name "rattle", for instance, stands for a group of experiences which have a common quality. This is classification. Grouping and classification leads to generalizing, or abstracting that which holds these experiences together as a class. The name doesn't necessarily stand for any single idea but rather for the idea of all similar ideas. Thus the word "rattle" stands for the idea which all rattles have in common. It defines an object with certain limited characteristics and which obeys certain limited rules. When using it the child has pooled a number of sense impressions. His sense impressions have grown into clear ideas. The quality of these ideas depends on the intensity and variety of the experiences which preceded them and with which they will continue to be associated.

At quite an early age the child begins to recognize the power of words. She utters an anguished "ma-ma" and her mother appears. By using the word "ballie" in an appealing tone she can persuade even the stranger to pick up her ball and give it to her every time she throws it over the pram. The word "No!" has tremendous possibilities.

As the child grows older and more articulate she finds in words a means of extending her exploration of the world, and between the ages of three and six she will pester attentive adults with questions. At a later stage she will seek her answers in books.

At all stages words offer the child opportunity and pleasure. He has every encouragement to develop his skill in using them. The complexities of becoming familiar with his mother tongue are conquered even by the child with little intelligence. Nearly all forms of human activity will involve him in words and if he fails to acquire them he fails as a human being. Few people fail in the early stages while learning language is part of living. It is later, when language is sometimes taught as a subject or attempts are made to isolate the study of it, that failure appears.

2

The development of speech

People communicate with one another in many ways: by facial expression and miming, by writing and speaking, by pictures, signs and diagrams and through the modes of expression employed in art. Most forms of communication involve the use of symbols, or vehicles expressing thoughts and feelings. By using symbols we are able to exchange ideas and impressions. While we are unable to transfer our ideas, we can at least convey information about them. Only human beings are able to do this.

Speech is the most widely used form of language and words are the units with which speech is structured. Words only become speech when they have meaning and stand for the objects they represent and when they are spoken so that they are comprehensible to others. The first noises a baby makes become speech when they are used to symbolize, when they are made intentionally and with meaning, and when they are understood by another person.

The baby is born with functioning speech organs: he cries, he babbles, and his vocal sounds are accompanied by gestures. He will only develop the use of speech, however, if he is reared amongst people who speak. He will acquire the language of those who speak to him.

Under normal circumstances a child learns to speak in the home. His ability to learn and the quality of his learning throughout his life depend considerably on the speech education he receives from his family. Most parents realize this and give the baby all the help they can. Fortunately they expect the child to accomplish speech naturally, and therefore they avoid hampering the child by their anxiety at this stage. Their faith in their child's ability to learn to speak is his greatest aid.

We will go back to Wendy and see what else was happening between her and her parents. From birth she was spoken to frequently during feeding, bathing, and so on. When she showed signs of trying to respond or imitate, single words or phrases were repeated. Her mother said, "She is allowed to put her fingers on our lips as we talk when she wants to as we feel it all helps her. Rhymes and nursery songs are often sung. She rocks and claps her hands and we joggle her up and down."

Sometimes Wendy would babble to herself. She seemed to listen to the sound she made and then repeat it. "Da....da...Ma...ma...Na...na". She would smile and wave her arms and legs in pleasure. She would respond with a smile when her mother spoke to her or even when she heard her mother's voice.

Following her use of the words "da-da" and "ma-ma", she added to her vocabulary "wow-wow" at nine months, "d'tee"(dirty) also at nine months, and at ten months "dodee" (dolly) and "teddy".

Sometimes these sounds were muddled unless an adult said the correct word first. Then she would correct herself in imitation. By this time she understood many things which were said to her and would respond to suggestions such as "Go and find your dolly". Later she would find things which were not in view.

She was nearly a year old before she added any new "words" to her vocabulary, but her passive (or understood) vocabulary had greatly increased by this time. It was as though she were consolidating what she had already learned. Much of her effort at this time went into standing and walking. Once these skills were accomplished her range of exploration was widened and her speech began to develop quickly.

She showed great interest in sounds of all descriptions. Listening to the clock she would say, "dee-dee". She liked to blow a recorder and make sounds such as "Bmm, click, yum-yum". "New" was adopted as the name of the cat, in spite of her parents' use of "Pussy".

By twelve months Wendy, an intelligent child with understanding parents, had established a foundation of sound patterns on which her speech could grow. Not only was she able to express her needs and show her approval to those who relieved them, she could use her speech sounds for pleasure. Learning her mother tongue gave her great delight.

Wendy's relationship with her parents was an important feature of he developing speech. They provided her with a pattern she could imitate; they tried to link her mind with theirs, and they shared the experience of speech with her and made it one she delighted in sharing.

Nicholas is barely seven weeks old. Already he opens his mouth when his parents speak to him. When they stop speaking he utters an encouraging crooning sound until they speak again. He smiles when they laugh and speak. Young as he is he seems to strive after speech. The emphasis is where it should be. The child is striving to accomplish a skill. His parents are trying to help him to do what he wants to do, rather than force on him something they want him to do. The whole experience is a great joy to all who participate.

The importance of the child's relationship with his parents cannot be overestimated. Where speech is concerned, the parents play a leading role. Children brought up in a normal family with attentive, interested parents appear to benefit. Institutionalized children tend to speak later, in spite of the loving devotion of the adults who rear them.

From the moment of birth, caring parents maintain a constant and close relationship with their baby. They use every possible means of communicating with him and encourage him in his endeavour to communicate by trying to understand and respond to his signals. They provide him with good word patterns. They use well-constructed sentences when they speak. Their voices modulate to convey meaning. Listening to them is a pleasure. They are patient with the child when he strives towards adult speech.

A baby understands many of the things said to him by people he knows well long before he uses intelligible words. Many infants will try to utter a series of sounds in imitation of sentence patterns before they say single words. Michael, aged twelve months, sat on his father's knee in the bus. He jabbered with great delight and his father responded as though holding a conversation. Mother asked in some surprise, "Can you tell what he says? I can't." "Neither can I," Father admitted. "But he wants you to answer him, so I do."

This kind of attention on the part of the adult affords children the best possible encouragement. The over-attentive adult, however, can hinder the development of speech. If children's needs are too often anticipated, they are not forced to express them. Children must need to verbalize and then earn the reward of adult understanding if they are to strive after speech.

Another important factor in speech development is the example of speech which surrounds children. Children who hear conversation between their parents and other members of the family have something to imitate. Their ability to say words is a skill which develops naturally, but their skill can only be exercised if their environment offers them the appropriate material.

Like other aspects of the child's development, speech follows an ordered pattern. All children go through the same sequence of stages, but the rate and quality of learning vary from child to child. In the early months of life babies communicate by means of crying, gesture, and simple sounds which later become babbling. Crying and gestures enable babies to communicate in a primitive way until their speech has developed. Babbling provides exercise for the organs of speech, and the physical ability to produce sounds and combine them is present long before a child is mentally ready. The association of meaning with word patterns must be present before we can use the term speech for the sounds made by children. Children have to learn how to arrange words into groups, or sentences before they can communicate adequately.

Children are good imitators. They catch their speech from the people they hear. A good model is essential and children will try hard to imitate faithfully. Much of what they hear reach their ears as a blurred, undulating pattern of sound. Children need the help of an adult if they are to learn to articulate correctly. Twins or children born close together tend to speak poorly, because they spend much time speaking to one another and their model is poor. The mature speech of the adult is essential as a good example.

When Judith was nearly two, her German cousin Johann, also two, came to live with her parents. The two children seemed to get on with one another and played together for much of their waking time. Each tried to imitate the other and eventually they created a unique language which each understood but which remained almost completely unintelligible to adults around them. It wasn't until they went to school and made independent friends that this language was abandoned and Johann learned to speak English.

Once a child has learned to speak he can communicate with others and, equally important, he can communicate with himself. As adults we usually do this inwardly, but the young child will often talk to himself aloud. He is equally happy to talk to inanimate objects.

When she was nearly two, Kathy's parents moved to a new bungalow. During the first few days Kathy spent much time by herself, trotting from door to door in the hall and pointing: "Atta cakie." (That is the kitchen, i.e. where I have a cake.) "Atta keen a teet." (That is the bathroom where I clean my teeth.) "Atta Kakie ded." (That is Kathy's bedroom.) "Atta Ma-ma." (That is mother's bedroom.) She was identifying familiar landmarks in her new home by naming them to herself.

In a good home children are encouraged to chatter. When possible they are included in adult conversation. They are talked to and listened to and parents know intuitively that this early chatter is the basis of learning. When children enter school their opportunities for chatter are extended. Teachers no longer consider the silent classroom to be a symbol of good control and their children are no longer denied their most effective means of discovering, through speech, what the world and the people who live in it are about.

3

How words acquire meaning

Sound patterns only become words when they have meaning. Words can be articulated without becoming part of speech. We can train a parrot to articulate, but only a human being can fill these sounds with meaning. Human speech is the unification of thought and sound, and in meaning we see the relationship between thought and speech.

The child has to learn to attach meaning to words. Furthermore, he has to learn that not only must a word mean something to him but the meaning he associates with it must be much the same as the meaning other people associate with the same word. A child will be brought up amongst people whose experiences are similar to his own. As a result his concepts and the words which symbolize them will be similar to those of the people with whom he communicates. The police officer's son, for instance, will attach a particular meaning to the term "beat".

Saying a word is only a stage in the child's growing awareness. The use of a vocal symbol crystallizes experience and thought, but the ultimate meaning attached to that symbol is not limited to what the child understands when he first uses it. Further experience, and reflection on experience, will continue to enrich the word with further meaning.

Consider the word "blanket", for instance. The baby in her pre-speech stages knows a good deal about her blanket. She knows the comforting warmth of it around her and the distressing cold if it falls away. She knows its roughness against her tongue and the queer smell of it when she has sucked it. She learns to recognize it under different guises. It can be pink or blue, big and thick or thin and light. Other people use blankets. There is a huge one when she goes into bed beside mother and father.

At a certain stage in her understanding the word "blanket" attaches itself to all these different experiences. She may recognize the spoken word "blanket" as meaning all of these things, even before she utters the sound herself she is led through meaning to the word.

Once she has acquired the word in speech it stands for her experiences and becomes verbal thought. But saying the word "blanket" is neither the beginning nor the end of knowing it, for meaning will be added as she meets blanket in fresh situations. As adults, for example, we now know electric blankets and Acrilan and Courtelle blankets. As long as we live we get to know more about the words we already use, and the words we use link us with early experience.

When a child first uses a word in speech the meaning he associates with it may be very limited. At eleven months Wendy associated "baby" with a picture on a cereal box. Soon she began to associate "baby" with any picture of people and with herself. This was a very happy experience. Supported by mother's delight in her achievement, she proceeded to say "baby" for every object, even those she had already named.

At about the same time, Wendy was brought face-to-face with another child of the same age. She touched it and called it "baby". She seemed to expect it to behave like her reflection in the mirror. When it began to babble independently, she was frightened and pulled away.

At twelve months Wendy used the word "truck" for her own wooden truck but not for the wooden truck belonging to another child. Eight months later, she used the word "two" for her own two shoes. After that she called any group of objects "two".

When a child comes into school he has acquired a vocabulary of about 10 000 words. He will double this before he leaves the primary school. He has picked up these words from adults and will start to use them as soon as he can attach any meaning to them. He can't wait until he has acquired the adult range of their meaning. It is very easy to assume that if a child uses a word correctly in a particular situation he has grasped the full range of its meaning.

A child may use such mathematical terms as "fast" and "slow", associating speed with them. Talking to him about speed soon reveals the fact that for him the word "speed" means "going fast like we do on the highway". It may have something to do with the shape of a speed car, but he is quite unable to connect it with his idea of slow. He has no concept at all of velocity.

When he uses the word "round" he means round like

a ball. He has yet to learn that it can mean round like a penny or a cocoa-tin , that the equator goes round the world, and that when we "round off" an object we make it smooth, and, later still, that a "round dozen" means full.

In one primary school a group of six-year-old children were interested in shapes. Material provided by the teacher helped to extend this interest and the children were awakened to the shape of the things they handled. One child brought a huge tricorn shell. It was filthy and had been lost amongst the rubbish in the attic since his father brought it back from the war. The interest in shape in the school had helped the child to recognize its possibilities.

The boy washed his shell and polished it. He felt its hardness. His fingers slipped inside the smooth hollow. "It must be lovely to live inside there," he murmured. "It would keep all the sea out." Then he enjoyed the design on the shell. With his finger he traced the curling pattern. "It goes round and round and round until it gets to nothing at the top", he reflected.

His teacher supplied the word "spiral" and he retraced the design. Now his body responded to the movement of his fingers. He was experiencing the idea of the spiral through the whole of his body. Later in the day, he and a group of his friends were found in a corner of the school cloakroom. They were performing a sequence of movements which they called their "Spiral Dance". They moved in complete silence and only their bodies expressed very eloquently their understanding of the word "spiral".

Later these children would recognize the spiral of a spring or a coil. When they met the word in print it would be rich with meaning. We could of course condition these same children at the age of five, or even three, to make the verbal response "spiral" every time we showed them the printed pattern. The fun of the game linked with adult approval would ensure the correct response at this stage. Later, however, when their thought processes matured, meaning would become essential to effective learning and these children would have some protection against the adult who required empty vocalizing from them. The teacher who provided the word "spiral" did so at the right time, when discovery had supplied enough meanings to form into an idea to which the word could be attached. She left the printed symbol representing the spoken word until later.

In this way, meaning attached to words comes from individual experience and varies from person to person. This is why we often find it extremely difficult to convey precisely our meaning to others. T.S. Eliot complains bitterly of the inadequacy of words as a vehicle of our thoughts:

> Words strain,
> Crack and sometimes break, under the burden,
> Under the tension, slip, slide, perish,
> Decay with imprecision, will not stay in place.
> Burnt Norton

Many of the child's first words are learned in the home, and meaning associated with them is often personal and within the context of the intimate life of the family. As an adult one frequently discovers that a familiar word meaning is not universal.

Much of what we know as meaning depends on the images words recall. The word "home" conjures very different images in people whose backgrounds differ widely. Even in a single country it may mean the image of a mansion in a park, a semi-detached house, an apartment unit, or a cottage. When we consider words which represent abstract ideas such as honesty, friendship, religion, and so on, the range of meaning is even greater.

Meaning also depends, of course, on the context in which a word appears. What does the simple word "blue" mean? It can be "out of the blue", "a blue joke", "feeling blue", "a blue dress", "the blue bag", "Oxford blue", "blue stocking". "Blue" itself means little until it becomes an instrument of speech, and the way in which it is used in a sentence gives us the clue.

Words are living links between the individual's inner world of ordered thought and his outer world of ordered experience. They exist only as they are in use and any help we give the child in learning about words can only be effective if we remember their living nature. Stripped of live meaning, words become empty symbols and as such have no use for the child.

4

Communication

Important as speech is, we must remember that it is not the only means of communicating thoughts and emotions. The child's education must include a wide variety of ways in which she can express her experiences, convey her impressions to others, and interpret the modes of expression used by other people.

The new-born baby depends considerably on crying as a means of expressing and conveying his needs and reactions. The baby's first cry assures us that he can breathe. He continues to cry, but his crying diminishes as his powers of speech develop. Crying is common to all babies and wherever they are born in the world they cry in the same way.

While parents expect their baby to cry, his crying often worries them, not so much because the sound is annoying as because it distresses them. Crying is associated with pain and unhappiness, and is often regarded as purely childish behaviour. Adults in our society, particularly male adults, are expected to avoid the use of tears to express feeling.

Parents respond to the expressive cries of their baby, and it is from this simple beginning that he learns to use vocal sounds, and later speech, as one means of communicating. But the baby of even a few weeks old uses other ways of making his needs known, such as wriggling when he is wet or smacking his lips when he is hungry, and if these signs are understood by his parents he will reserve his crying for more desperate situations.

Facial expressions and gestures accompany crying, but may be used independently. Again from such simple beginnings we get mime, sign-language, and the drama and dance of adult life. In ballet we find an artistic synthesis of all these forms of communication. When we watch a play or an opera, it is difficult for us to realize that all of this originated in the elementary movements and calls of the baby.

By the time the children enter school they will be using

most of the modes of communication available to human beings. Much of their time in school will be spent in developing these skills. We cannot develop the children's skill with words effectively if we neglect other aspects of their language development, and when we foster their use of many modes of expression we find that they all contribute to their verbal skill.

Very often we find that words permeate even their physical and artistic forms of language. An observer in a primary school is struck by the diversity and skill of six-year-old children in their use of communication and by the many aspects of their person that are employed in their exchanges with others.

One of the happiest sounds in the world is the uninhibited laughter of children. It is also highly expressive. It can range from the wicked glee of the child who has caused a flood in the cloakroom by blocking the toilet with soil to the sheer delight of the girl who has created a rainbow with the aid of a spray attached to a hose on a sunny day. A school for young children which rings with merriment is a place of active discovery and emotional satisfaction.

Sometimes the voices of the six-year-old children are silent. Their teacher is telling a story. She watches the faces of the children gathered at her feet. She knows that John understands the humour, that Peggy is identifying with the heroine, that George is puzzled because the story is a little beyond him, that Tina enjoys the thrill of fear, and that Ian's imagination has caught him up in a world beyond the sound of her words. Six-year-old children have not learned to dissemble and all they feel is conveyed by the expression on their faces.

Ming and Keith are building with bricks. They rarely speak as the edifice grows between them. Ming is the mastermind. She points and nods or frowns. Sometimes she snatches a brick impatiently. Keith watches and responds. Occasionally he pushes a brick forward tentatively, changing the shape of things, and gurgles with delight if Ming accepts the suggestion.

Play is well under way in the playhouse. Jill has got a scarf from the dressing-up corner. She ties it round her head and parades up and down with a basket, peddling imaginary pegs from door to door. She pauses by the pram and, with fingers arched like claws and her face screwed into a wizened leer, she casts a spell upon the babe.

Outside on the grass a number of children are moving in response to their individual use of percussion instruments. Peter with the castanets matches the sounds he makes with sharp, angular movements of his arms and legs and body. Dawn clashes the cymbals and leaps with the sound. Jenny has a musical box and her dance patterns are complicated as she weaves in circles round the box on the ground. All the children express in their own way the feeling stimulated by their own percussion sounds.

One group of children are making books at the writing-table. Very few words appear in the books, but a reader is left in no doubt as to what the child wants to say. Vicki's book, "My Family", conveys in vivid pictures exactly what she feels about her mother who smokes and has blackened teeth, her father who takes her to play on the swings in the park and Uncle George who is drawn with two heads because "Mother says he is two-faced".

Four children at another table are using fabric, feather and sequins with which to convey their impression of "what the queen looks like when she comes to Canada". Thoughtful Julie has given her a tiny red velvet wrist-bag "to carry pennies in for the 'Ladies'", and we realize her limited concept of the life of a queen.

Ali has a lump of clay. He pounds it relentlessly into a pancake and then proceeds to poke his fingers into the pliant surface. Quickly he destroys his pattern and squeezes the lump until his knuckles whiten. His teeth are clenched and we sense the powerful feelings which possess him. Eventually his fingers begin to stroke and smooth the emerging shape of a chubby puppy. With infinite care he details the eyes and the mouth, and then sits back in silent delight and stares at what he has made. He finds something of himself expressed by clay he has fashioned.

In schools where children are encouraged to live rich and varied lives, expressive behaviour is well developed and highly eloquent. Words may play a subsidiary or primary part, but they are not used in isolation. The children's use of speech is thus enriched and their words are embodied in all they experience. Children cannot acquire skill in the use of words if they are isolated and dealt with in the form of "speech training", drilling recognizing words in print, spelling lists, and the like. Long before children can benefit from systematic teaching in word usage, they must develop their natural skill in communication. School offers children the unique opportunity to communicate with other children and with adults who belong to the world outside the family.

Many of our children come into school with very

inadequate modes of expression. The exchange of words in conversation is something they may never experience in the home. In the liberal atmosphere of a primary school children are encouraged to talk to one another as often as to the teacher. Indeed, school is a place where children should do far more talking than the teacher. It is here that many of our children learn to converse through their exchanges with their friends.

Susie, aged five, is wearing a new dress made of pretty blue cotton with crisp white frills. She is anxious to secure the attention of her friend, Maria.

Susie: "I've got a new dress. My Mum made it. The frills took hours and hours and she says it looks 'spensive'."

Maria: "What's 'spensive'?

Susie: 'spensive'...'spensive'... it costs a lot of money"

Maria: "My Mum's got lots and lots of dresses. She goes out when I've gone to bed. She goes dancing and she looks like those dancing ladies on TV".

Susie: "I don't care about your Mum. I've got a new dress and I'm going to show it to Mr. C. " (teacher)

Listening to this exchange of words, one could scarcely call it conversation. Each child is pursuing her own line of thought with little reference to what the other is thinking. These children are highly egocentric in their behaviour and the social graces have yet to develop.

Roy is six and a half. He rushes into school and seeks out his friend, Andrew with great excitement.

"Our Mike (his big brother) gave me a dollar for cleaning his bike. So I'd enough money and I've been to Woollies and got a battery. We can fix that robot with eyes that light up."

Andrew catches Roy's enthusiasm. "Super! We'll get that wire stuff from the make-box and we'll ask Mr. C. for some bulbs."

While these two boys are working together on their robot, their verbal exchange is interlaced with a number of other forms of communication.

"These bulbs have to fit in here." Roy wiggles them into sockets (bulb-holders) fixed in their cardboard box robot. They won't stay in place.

"Here!" Andrew has a go. He uses a scrap of adhesive tape. "There!" He looks to Roy for approval and is rewarded with a grin: "They'll work like this." Andrew dramatizes a robot. He glides along the floor and indicates with his fingers how the eyes will flash. He returns to the cardboard model and stares from the bulbs to the battery. "Can you fix the wire?" he asks Roy.

Roy assumes the attitude of the expert and Andrew stands by full of confidence. The bulbs flicker and Andrew thumps Roy on the back. In silence they work together. Andrew obliges by holding bulb-holders and pieces of wire, while Roy fiddles expertly. Glancing at Roy's face from time to time Andrew anticipates his friends needs and the job is completed. The master-minds now carry their robot from room to room so that all shall appreciate its flashing eyes. Outbursts of dramatic action greet the robot and "They must be exterminated", "We must be vitalized," ring out all over the school.

Many forms of communication are employed in activities of this kind. Children who know one another well will paint a picture together, share the construction of models, or weave a pattern in dance together. Sometimes not a word is spoken. The medium itself provides a channel through which they can share a common experience.

Like other aspects of learning at this stage, communication is a total experience. By encouraging the child to use language in all its diversified forms we foster the full development of each mode of communication for his later use.

5

The use of symbols

The child inherits a world where symbols of all kinds play a leading part. Human beings use a wide range of symbols and everyday life depends on the individual's skill in using them. In sharing the world of their parents, children meet these symbols and see their parents using them wherever they go and whatever they do.

We use maps and diagrams, pictures and photographs, road signs and signals, notes and numbers and words, morse code and other forms of sign language, models and braille, toys, patterns, plans, hand-signals. We also use many artistic forms of symbolism in the shape of dance, drama, story, and so on.

We reduce the world to a form of shorthand by making simple signs stand for the real thing. The symbols are convenient and more easily handled than objects and the experiences they represent. While symbols serve our purposes, they frequently do us a disservice. They can be misinterpreted, and this leads to confusion. Sometimes they are misleading. A boy of seven seeing a live cow for the first time gasped: "I never thought cows were that big." Two-dimensional paper pictures are poor substitutes for a living animal.

When we use a symbol it reminds us of a previous experience. We recall things and situations, or feelings which are no longer there. By so doing we can make use of previous experience in a new situation. This is the foundation of reasoning and problem-solving, a means by which we can apply what we have learned to help us to adjust to a fresh set of circumstances.

We begin to develop this skill at a very early age. The baby of five or six months will watch her mother hide her ball under a cushion, and although she cannot see it she will feel under the cushion and retrieve the ball with a squeal of delight.

She can use a mental image as a substitute for the real thing.

Michael was two and a half when his aunt got him from home to take him out. At the door Michael stopped and asked: "Is it a long way?" His aunt nodded. "Yes" she explained. "We're going to see Grandma. We'll go on the bus." Michael let go of her hand. He ran back to the kitchen, opened the pantry door, cut a slice from the chocolate cake on the shelf and wrapped it in a paper napkin. Last time he'd been taken to Grandma's on the bus he'd felt hungry before he arrived. He was using past experience not merely to solve an immediate problem but to anticipate a possible emergency and solve it in advance.

No doubt at this stage Michael's experiences were stored in his mind in the shape of images as much as in words. As his use of words increased he learned to rely more on verbal symbols than on pictorial ones. As adults we solve many problems by talking them out to ourselves.

When we use a symbol we do not need to recall, one by one, all the experiences which gave that symbol meaning. We can step straight on from the stage that symbol represents. Take the case of the word "bottle". Long before we recognized the word we had been gathering experiences to provide it with meaning. We knew the bottle from which we first had milk. After that stage the milk came in a straight-shaped container. We knew the hard, smooth feel of glass, the warmth of it full of milk, and the satisfaction of the sweet milk filling an empty stomach. On the dressing table there were other kinds of bottles containing a number of things. Another collection of bottles was in a cupboard. The grocery bottles were different again and in the drug stores were bottles of many colours, shapes and sizes. Now when we say the word "bottle" or see a printed word-pattern "bottle" we know that it represents the characteristics common to all bottles. We have learned to extract those features which all bottles have in common. This process of abstraction leads to an idea and the bottle symbol reminds us of our idea. We can use our idea without referring back to all the bottles we have met. It is on such mental activities that understanding is based and intellect develops.

It is more convenient to carry a picture around for reference than to carry the object that picture represents. It is even more convenient to carry a word, or an idea, in the mind. Human beings then dispense with concrete objects and situations as soon as they can. The ideas he has in his mind go with him in a very compact form wherever he goes. Words and ideas require neither space nor transport facilities. Once we have acquired a wealth of ideas or concepts, we can gear up towards new concepts and concepts of a higher order. We then see for instance, bottles as belonging to a class of objects called vessels and then vessels as part of a class of objects called utensils and so on.

Children in the primary school are dealing with many types of symbols. We provide them with a wealth of real objects and with the opportunity to consolidate their experiences of them, before we expect them to deal with the symbols alone. Ultimately we want them to acquire adult skill in using abstract ideas and symbols but we know that the quality of their thoughts and the meaning they attach to symbols depend on full personal acquaintance with the concrete situations behind the abstractions.

Children realize that adults play with these intellectual toys (words, numbers and signs of all kinds). They want to know about them and also to be able to play with them. Symbols intrigue them and they will make every effort to master symbols and acquire skill in using them if we give them the chance. If, however we thrust the symbols upon them too soon, if we try to make them memorize the symbols and tell them what they stand for before children have a chance to gather their information through experience, then we spoil the children's chance for full understanding, and the symbols may become empty of meaning and difficult to handle.

While children are gathering personal information from the real environment, they are growing familiar with the symbols which permeate an articulate society. They notice that there are numbers on birthday cards, on the pages of a story book, on the board at school, and on the lunch money they take to school. There are printed words on packets of paste, on bottles of cough medicine, on notices the teacher makes, in books, on records and in the back of a new coat. There are diagrams showing how to make an experiment, and maps of a globe which tell them about the world. There are note symbols in the song book and paper patterns which show how to cut out a doll's dress. There are pictures and photographs and sometimes films which show them things they have never seen. Always, of course there are spoken words and they are everywhere all the time.

Some of these symbols are easier than others to recognize. Even so, the child's interpretation of them depends on the concrete experiences he can associate with them. A film tells him more than a photograph about a kangaroo. The photograph tells him more than a picture but nothing can tell him about the soft feel of the kangaroo's fur better than his own fingers. If we want the child to gain a concept of Africa, we bring him real drums and skins and utensils and put them into his hands before we show him pictures which extend his own impressions.   In spite of the complexity of our use of symbols, children rarely confuse the various classes of symbols, even before they understand them. They know which symbols represent notes or words, numbers or shapes. Once their interest is aroused and they become aware of the various signs, they seem able to classify them from the start. Symbols are amongst many other of their discoveries. In ordering the world, the child learns to classify symbols as naturally as he learns to classify objects. They are all part of a vast complexity of things he has the urge to explore and ultimately to fit into a pattern.

Of all our symbols, words are the most challenging. Many people think of education in school mainly as a means of instructing the child in the use of words. "Grammar" schools would seem to be reserved for that purpose. While accepting this as a teacher's most important responsibility, we must not think that we can isolate verbal education. As in all aspects of child development, children will only grow in verbal understanding as a part of their total growth. We know that they need to explore social relationships, to feel and respond, to move with their hands, their body and their mind to discover what life is about, what they are and what they are doing here. The effects of education are evident in the whole person.

In spite of this we measure the effects of education by the child's verbal skill. Only in special circumstances do we attempt to assess creative ability, mechanical skill, physical competence, or social maturity. Assessment of the personality is often secondary to academic attainment.

The bulk of our children are assessed by examinations which require the children to read, understand and interpret questions and to answer them either on paper or by spoken word.   Entrance to a career as an adult is first by paper qualifications which record the result of verbal examinations. Usually a personal interview decides the suitability of a candidate, but it rarely precedes written examination.

We need not quarrel with this procedure if we avoid letting it distort the idea we have of education. The child who has been allowed to develop as fully as possible in every aspect will stand up to being measured in any one of those aspects. We must, in other words, know precisely what examinations assess and whether that is what we want to assess.

Most important of all the teacher must keep examinations in perspective. We don't orient our work towards them. Children living the full life of the moment ensure their own future. If we want them to become articulate as adults, we must give them time and opportunity to play with water, to put their finger under the tap, to pour water, splash it, swim in it and drink it, to observe its behaviour in every way possible, before we drill them into recognizing drip, dribble, gush, flow and squirt in speech or in print.

We need to remember, too, that significant as words are they are not the only means by which an individual can become articulate. Indeed, many ideas and feelings are more adequately expressed through body movement or creative work, and the young learner should have access to symbolism in all its various guises in order to develop really adequate powers of communication. To limit the children's education to a study of words is to limit their powers of development, and their world will only become fully intelligible if they are able to translate the many types of symbols used in representing our impressions of it. Education in communication involves the exercise of the full range of the child's capacity to experience and respond.

6

Words and thought

Piaget devoted a lifetime to investigating the ways in which children think and reason. He warns us against assuming that because a child seems to learn to talk like adults she has learned to think like them. In examining the child's verbal facade, Piaget shows us how the structuring of the child's thought-processes follows a progression of stages. He emphasizes the slow, inward, evolutionary growth of the child's mind as an aspect of the child's total growth.

The development of thought is seen by Piaget and his co-workers as the result of continuous interaction between the child and environment. The process is twofold. The child endeavours on the one hand to fit information she gains from experience into the developing world within herself, and on the other hand to modify her behaviour so that she fits into the developing world outside herself.

In the early stages these two processes operate side by side. Eventually they fuse and become aspects of the child's mental life. It is through the use of language and in her relationships with other people that the child comes to realize that hers is not the only point of view, that all she finds in the world is not only related to her but to other people as well, and that she must give as well as receive and so become part of the great human complex.

As these developments take place, the child is also learning how to store her external experiences in the form of thought. Not only can she store her impressions as ideas, she can recall them, relate them and manipulate them. She can reflect, use previous experience in existing circumstances, and even deal with hypothetical situations. This process provides the foundation for intellectual growth.

Piaget was a biologist, and this training may have strongly influenced his point of view, but an observer of children sees much in their behaviour which confirms his findings. His views have certainly helped teachers to understand the many problems associated with the way in which children think and learn. People who live in close contact with children can observe for themselves the way in which a child converts experiences into images she can retain as part of her mental structure, or in the terms Piaget uses, the way in which she internalizes her actions.

Katherine, aged six months, was sitting on the carpet facing a chair. Father was amusing her by playing "peek-a-boo", from behind the chair. After the game had proceeded for a few minutes, whenever father disappeared Katherine waited in suppressed mirth until his head reappeared at the far end of the chair. She expected his face to appear because she could recall her impressions of a few moments earlier.

At twelve months, if Katherine was given a spoon she would scramble into her high-chair. Just holding a spoon in her hand reminded her of what she did with food placed in a bowl on the tray of her chair.

When two-year-old Christopher is tired of walking, he will lift up his arms to his father and say, "Carry-up!" He has experienced the relief of what happens when father says, "I'll pick him up and carry him". Not only can he recall the experience, he is using it to solve his immediate problem.

When three-year-old Susie was given two wrapped toffees by her aunt she put one of them in her pocket, murmuring "Tomorrow". Susie had reached the stage when she could anticipate a future event.

In the next garden, two four-year-old children were talking. Anita said, "We're taking a picnic in the park today."

Vicki enquired, "How do you know?"

"Well" explained Anita, "Yesterday Daddy said we would go tomorrow and now tomorrow is today, isn't it?"

Her powers of reasoning were well developed.

In school, as we watch young children learning we observe the internalizing process hourly. John, the new arrival finding his way around the school, is shown by his teacher how to identify his classroom door. "This is my name on the door," she points out. "Miss Wetheringham is a long name. Just look for the door with the longest name". John is five and he cannot read, but he can retain the mental picture of the longer pattern her name makes and knows his classroom door from all the others which look alike.

Vesna is setting the table in the playhouse. Gary and

Win and John are coming for tea. She gets a handful of plates from the shelf and hopes for the best. When she has a set for each person she has a few plates left over and puts these back. A week or so later she has devised a more economical procedure. She gets plates one at a time, one for Gary, one for Win, one for John, and one for Vesna. It will be some months perhaps before she can visualize the expected number of places and get the appropriate number of plates in one operation.

Derek is making a model steamboat and the funnel must stand up straight. Shaping it from a discarded toilet-roll container is a difficult job. Paste dabbed round the rim at the bottom won't work. He manages eventually to achieve his purpose by using strips of adhesive tape. Derek then makes a second funnel and this time he cuts the bottom like teeth and bends them outwards to provide place for his paste.

Sally is experimenting with the balance pans. She has a collection of small objects (dog-biscuits, thread bobbins, pegs, beads, etc) in a cookie tin and a box containing grams and other standard weights. She spends a considerable amount of time with the small objects alone, piling things into the pans until she sees the indicator point straight up and down.

She then selects all the little wooden pegs from among her objects. She puts dog-biscuits and thread-bobbins in one pan and pegs one by one in the other until the two balance. A few days later she takes one of the weights (100 grams) and balances the gram weights against it. She carries on with this experiment using a number of different weights.

Two weeks later a group of children are baking. "It says .5 kg of flour, a .25 of butter....," one child says, reading out the recipe. Sally goes straight to the weights and selects three. "This is .5 kg. , this is .25 of a kilogram and that's five grams," she says. "I know because I've tried them"

Step by step, Sally memorized her actions until eventually they became fused into thought. She could now dispense with early exploratory action and use the idea which had come to represent those actions.

Even as adults we need to go through much the same process when faced with an unfamiliar situation. Learning to drive a car is a concrete learning problem many adults face. We need to handle the shifter physically before we have a mental impression of our actions when changing gears.

There is obviously a close connection between the activity of thinking and the use of words. As we think we seem to talk to ourselves inwardly. We cannot, however, say that thought and speech are the same things. Indeed, we often find great difficulty in putting our thoughts into words. Thoughts struggle to take shapes we can recognize and words help us to translate thought into familiar forms.

Often as children explore and experiment they can be heard talking to themselves. This seems to help them in making their discoveries. Putting their actions into words helps them to understand and internalize. Thought can be seen as action stored in the form of words. Sometimes as adults we use verbalizing as an aid to action. When we are packing for a holiday, for example, we tell ourselves aloud what to put into the suitcase. When we fit the pieces of a dress pattern over a length of material we argue aloud as to the most advantageous arrangement. Children feel the need to do this more often than adults.

Keith is packing the bricks into their storage box. "If I put the big ones in first," he tells himself, "I can fill the bits at the side with little ones ... These two moon shapes fit together and those squares just go on top of this long one. Miss C. said those weren't squares. The sides were squares. They're cubes. And the long one is called an oblong..."

If the development of children's thought-processes is so much a matter of inward growth and maturation, does what we do with them in school make any difference? Will they grow intellectually, irrespective of the environment we provide? Is the enriched life we offer them in school going to help them to develop their ideas sooner or develop concepts of a higher quality?

Developing concepts sooner will not necessarily mean that children will be more intelligent or go further in their thinking as adults. The quality of ideas is more important than the speed in going through the stages. The quality of learning depends on the amount of effort the child puts into it. What we can do is make the child want to learn and this is our first aim when preparing for learning situations in school. The degree of interest for the child in what we offer will determine the enthusiasm he or she brings to the job. This is the secret of good teaching: to stimulate the desire to be taught. We realize, too, that a wide range of situations to explore will add meaning to the words and ideas the child acquires. Words full of meaning provide enriched material for the stuff of thoughts. These thoughts are a synthesis of the child's inward experience and of the experiences found in the outer world.

Children's understanding of both themselves and the

world grows as an aspect of their total development. As they acquire an ever-widening vocabulary of words to represent their stored experiences their mental powers mature and they become increasingly more capable of using symbolic processes. Children alone can make the effort to acquire the skill of thought and understanding. All we can do is provide them with first-class opportunities and then allow them all the time they need.

7

Words and personality

We no longer believe that a child inherits his personality. He may inherit certain temperamental and physical characteristics, and intelligence has much to do with innate ability, but the way in which this basic material will develop into the child's personal pattern depends on how and what he learns. As he grows older he may resemble his father or mother because he has used them as a pattern on which to model himself. He has become like them by imitating their behaviour and adopting their attitudes. He depends on them almost entirely during his most formative years, and they play a leading role in the development of his individual personal pattern.

Language in its many forms provides the link between the child and other people. Through communicating with others the child finds out about other people and about himself, but before he can do this he must become aware of himself as a separate person.

During his first months the baby moves his limbs and body about. He explores the shape of himself with his hands and finds out where he stops and the world outside himself begins. As he becomes more aware of his separate existence and realizes that he is a different person from the parent who feeds him and cares for him, the approval or disapproval of that other person helps him to learn what sort of a person he is. He wants to please the person he depends on, if only to secure the satisfaction of his needs. He knows from mother's reactions which of the things he is doing pleases her (the "Yes" things) and which do not (the "No" things).

Even though he doesn't understand mothers' words at this early stage, the child knows the difference between "Good boy" and "Bad boy", if only by the tone of her voice and the emotional message he receives from her. Once he has acquired words for himself, learning about self goes ahead quickly. He finds that, in his turn, he can register approval or disapproval of others, to which they respond. Most parents have experienced their child's discovery and delight in the power of "No".

The fact that he can manipulate others and make them respond to him helps the child to become increasingly aware of himself. He is then in a position to get to know that self. The first two years of his life are an extremely important period of personal development. We know from the evidence of deaf children, whose language is impaired, how handicapped they are without the use of words.

Normally a child of two will know his own a name. He can label himself and he alone bears that particular label. He can use his name to refer to himself and others understand. When Kathie, aged two years and one month, had finished her pudding she would say, "Good Kaffie". If she were reprimanded she would murmur, "Kaffie gone". By the time she was three she had developed much further her powers of self-identification. One day she was trying to sweep the yard with an enormous brush and father came to her rescue. Kathie clung determinedly to the brush and scowled. "Do it afelf", she asserted.

Some children even on entering school are unable to apply the pronoun words to themselves. Although they are well able to say "me", mine" etc., and will even understand what the adult means when he refers to "your so-and-so", they get very confused when it comes to using these substitutes for their own name. Tony, aged five and a half, tried to reason this out.

"You said that it (a tidy box) was 'yours' and that means it's Tony's." His teacher nodded: "When you talk about that box you say, 'It is mine' or 'my box'." To which Tony replied, "So yours is the same as mine." A week later the penny had dropped and Tony took great delight in labelling all that was "mine".

The development of the child's self-idea is a twofold process. She finds out, on the one hand, what idea other people have of her by what they say to her and about her. At the same time she discovers what she is like through experiences such as using materials which provide her with adequate opportunity for self-expression. The child sees in her own work and in the finished product something of herself. Likewise, when she tries to use father's hammer or to run like big sister, more of herself is revealed.

By the time she is two the child has established at least

an awareness of the bodily self. With the aid now of language, she can label herself "Karen". She can now understand that when people use her name, "Karen is a good girl", and "Karen has ten little toes", "This is for Karen", they see her as a separate entity. When they use her name she can attach the things they say to herself. Her name identifies and it remains extremely significant to her for the rest of her life.

It is important for the child to develop a favourable but authentic idea of herself and her abilities. She must learn to accept and like herself before she can learn to accept and like others. On the other hand she must know her limitations, for if her levels of attainment are set too high she will feel a failure and be unable to adjust to life as it is.

The idea of what she is as a physical person provides the anchorage for her psychological self. First her parents and family and then friends of the family will tell her what she is like. "Billy is tall for his age." "You've got a good-looking boy here". "Bill's going to be a proper little tear-about". "You're going to be a wow with the girls, Billy. Just like your father." The mirror confirms this message and Billy gains respect for this bodily self which is to serve him for the whole of his life.

Not all children, of course, gain a favourable impression of self. "Just look at the ugly little brat! Screaming his head off", "You get those legs from your Uncle Tom, Jimmy. None of your mother's side are like that." The handicapped child particularly needs very special help.

Ideas of bodily self are interwoven with self-ideas which are not only physical. The "good boy" refers to something inside the bodily self. "He's a clever little boy, he is." "Our Billy's ahead of his age. Perhaps he'll get to university." "Give Judy one of your candies, Billy. Be kind to her when she comes to play with you." "Billy's such a happy child!"

At the same time Billy is trying to explore other selves, often by imitating what interests him in other people. He pretends to be a parent and wants a basket to carry things in at the supermarket. He gets under the table and barks like a dog. He puffs around the subway station platform and his curiosity is so intense that he becomes that train for the time being. In this way he discovers that things have no selves, but that people have selves and that he can graft parts of those selves on to his own.

When the child comes into school his opportunities are widened. This may be the first time he has encountered at close quarters children of his own age. They will soon prove to him that life isn't centred in his feelings and needs, that he will have to develop as deep an awareness of others as he has of himself. Teachers and other adults in the school will further confirm his realistic view of himself and help him to adjust his own demands so that he can fit in with others. By this time much of his exchange with other people takes place in the form of words.

Jeremy started school on his fifth birthday. He brought a handful of birthday cards and his new tractor. His teacher welcomes him. "Hello! You're Jeremy, aren't you? You look a big sensible boy, and I'm going to give you a special job. We have two lots of birthday cards today. Would you like to stand them up on this table and then we'll show them to the other boys and girls."

Feeling important, Jeremy forgot his initial apprehension. He put his tractor on the floor and set to work on the cards. Peter, an established member of the group, admired the tractor. "How does it tip up?" He crouched down to investigate.

Jeremy paused, torn between his desire to complete his important job and his urge to protect his tractor. He went on with his job but kept a vigilant eye on Peter's investigations. Peter fumbled. "Don't think it works," he muttered in disgust.

"Does!" Jeremy hastened to demonstrate. "If we'd got some dirt, I'd show you." Peter pointed through the classroom window "There's dirt out there" he said. "We can go out when it isn't raining." Jeremy assumed the role of leadership. "I'll show you," he offered. "And you can help." Fresh aspects of his personality were opening up.

Through these early years the child explores any materials which come his way. With effort and patience he discovers that he has power over materials, he can find out what they will do, and then he can make them serve his purpose. As a result of his manipulation there is often an end-product and this provides visible evidence of what he can do and what he is like. His end-product differs from the end-product of others. It is as unique to him as his personality is.

Jane, aged three, was given a piece of pastry dough to keep her busy until the baking was finished. Jane kneaded, rolled and shaped it, and her finished cookies went into the oven. Her biscuits were clearly different from her mother's. Her aunt coming into the kitchen, said, "Are these Jane's cookies? I'll have one of these. They're a funny shape but they're scrumptious. You're going to be a good cook, Jane."

When Jane came into school she spent hours handling

clay. Even after she had made her initial discoveries she was contented to knead it and pummel it, making a shape and then squeezing it out of existence. One day she sat in front of her lump of clay completely absorbed, watching it shape under her fingers.

"I'm going to make a man," she murmured. "I'll squeeze out this piece for his head...Now he must have some arms...and some legs..." She talked as she worked and eventually sat back.

"I've made you," she smiled at her clay man. "I must give you a name because you're a real man. You're Bumps." In her role of creator she had implanted a grain of herself in what she created and therefore she loved it. Having created it, she named it and so confirmed its existence.

In the crude creative work of our children we see much of what they are as people. Listening to children's creative use of words, in the form of speech, provides us with the best clue to their personalities. Later they will also learn to put these things on paper.

Anne was happily absorbed in painting. "I'm going to paint my house blue, because it's quiet like the sky. When I'm big I'll have a room with a blue carpet and blue paper on the wall. It'll be pretty and smell nice and nobody will shout." It was easy for the teacher who observed this activity to catch a glimpse of Anne as an adult. In a few words Anne revealed the idea of herself which would influence her development towards adult personality.

As adults we may learn much about another person from their appearance and from the way they behave, but it is often in conversation that we reach through to their innermost thoughts. Words play an important part in the development of a personality pattern, and the way in which we use our words is highly indicative of our personality.

8

Playing with symbols

By symbols we mean emblems which represent something else. Our use of symbols depends on common agreement as to the meaning of the emblem we use.

The idea of letting one thing stand for another develops at a very early stage and we can watch in children their progression towards the use of symbols. Jason at eighteen months was turning the pages of a picture book with his father. A large golden pear on one page attracted his attention. He pretended to pick it from the page and put it into his mouth. He then went through the book, repeating the procedure with other pictures of fruit. He knew that the picture stood for the real object.

Janet's favourite game at the age of four was playing restaurant. She needed few properties and would use stones or leaves for plates, food, even people. Sometimes she dispensed with real objects altogether and would use action alone in place of them.

At a very early age children like to make marks on paper. By the time they are three they can use many kinds of media and will scribble with pencil and charcoal or paint and crayon. Three-year-olds will try, in two-dimensional pictures, to represent things they have seen. By making two-dimensional pictures represent their impression of three-dimensional objects they perform a considerable feat. A study of children's scribble reveals some interesting features. There is a strong resemblance in the symbol for a person whichever human race the child belongs to. There would seem to be a sequence of stages, too, in the development of the picture from the ball-and-stick person of the three-year-old to the detailed figure in profile of the nine-year-old child.

Amongst these early scribblings the child will include letters and numbers, road-signs and notes. The seven-year-old may even try to draw a diagrammatic view of a street or perhaps a "map of my way to school". Sometimes children will know what their symbols stand for. Sometimes they will tell the onlooker incorrectly what they are supposed to represent. Sometimes they will ask, "What does this say?"

Understanding of different types of symbols does not come to children in any particular order. They don't necessarily learn to recognize words before maps or numbers before notes. As their thought-processes become more definitely structured and their capacity for dealing with the abstract develops, the idea of our use of symbols grows.

Right from their early recognition of symbols children begin to discriminate between the kinds of symbols which represent words, numbers, notes, road-signs, songs. They never try to represent a song by using numbers. As their powers of discrimination develop they begin to recognize the differences between symbols of the same type, as between word patterns for example. If we urge them too soon to discriminate between word patterns, they start to become confused, lose confidence and may even grow to fear the very symbols which have been their toys until the adult spoiled their game. Children's natural curiosity is very great. Once they are familiar with symbols, they are extremely anxious to interpret them. They delight in their own discoveries. Why, in our anxiety, do we tend to rush them and turn their joy into apprehension, and then blame them because they flounder?

The child's world is permeated by these symbols and they meet them hourly as a part of everything they are doing. They associate them with their emotional and physical state at the time of contact. Amidst the excitement of going on holiday he meets the symbol which stands for the road on Daddy's map. He knows the symbol on the clock which indicates dinnertime, the number on his card which says he is five, the notes which stand for "Happy Birthday to You". He can discriminate between "Push" and "Pull" on the swing doors. He knows what arrows mean and the road-sign which says "No Entry".

The symbols children meet are just as exciting as any other of their discoveries. They enjoy playing with them and speculating about their meaning. They are free to interpret them as they decide and the meaning they attach at this stage is their personal decision. These symbols will remain his or her friends until the adult starts to isolate them from the pleasurable experiences the child associates with them, and so to divorce them of meaning. It is the adult who reduces the child's handling of symbols to a form of drill or even of drudgery.

Children's interest in symbols is a natural stage in their growing concept of the world. In their own good time they will need the help of the adult to interpret them precisely and use them with skill. Adults often fail them by their lack of confidence in their natural aptitude for development. They can create in a the child positive distaste for symbols and a lack of confidence in dealing with them.

Amongst the many symbols employed by a literate society, numbers play a highly important role. They represent the ordering of the universe. Again young children perform a tremendous feat in reducing their experiences to mathematical order.

Mary loved playing with mother's button-box. At the age of four she would gather together those which were similar in some way. She was probably unaware that they had any particular quality in common; they simply seemed to go together. A few weeks later she approached the activity with a particular criterion in mind. "I'll have all the red ones here...all the blue ones...the big ones...the small ones...the big blue...the little red...", and, later still, even such refinements as "the big blue with two holes" and so on.

In school children manipulate much of their material in this way. All the big blocks are assigned to one end of the box. Bricks are sorted according to shape or colour or purpose. At a certain stage number becomes a significant quality of groups. Many groups have the quality of five or three, or two. From all such similar groups the idea of five, or three, or two is extracted. The idea then stands for all groups containing that number of objects.

The child is now ready to understand the sound of the word "five". It is at a later stage that the printed symbol 5 is recognized as standing for the experience of five. The symbol 5 is a precise and economical way of representing all the child understands from these experiences. He or she does not necessarily know yet that five comes after four and before six, or that the five group is the four group with one added. The child may be quite unaware that the adult has decided on a particular order for naming the symbols in sequence, "One, two, three, four, five". It may not be until he or she is six or seven that they are ready to count with any idea of what counting means.

Yet how often do we find the fond parent presenting her five-year-old son to a teacher with the assurance that "He can count. Show the teacher how you can count, Barry. One, two, three..." Sometimes, even teachers fall into the trap of believing that because the child is able to say and repeat these words he knows what counting means. He must know about groups and their names before he can put them in order and to see the relationship between them. In *Discovering the Physical World* we consider in greater detail the development of mathematical ideas and the use of mathematical symbols.

When talking to children and listening to what they say, we realize that they have acquired a great many terms and expressions before they come into school and that the meaning they attach to these terms is shallow and imprecise. One of the teacher's main responsibilities is to help children to enlarge the meaning of the terms they use and to use them more precisely. The most effective way of doing this is to provide extensive experiences and to encourage children to talk about these experiences.

A group of objects had been set out for the children to handle. One little girl picked up a glass paper-weight and admired it. "It's soft," she said appreciatively. This was an opportunity for the teacher to give her the word "smooth" and at the same time let the child handle and describe a number of objects which were either soft or smooth. Later she found objects such as fur and silk which were both soft and smooth.

David was trying to find a piece of wood which he and Ian could shape into an oar for their boat. He held a length in his hand. " This one won't do," he explained. "I want a piece that's a bit less long." Because he knew "short" when he spoke about his friend being a "short boy", it came as quite a surprise to his teacher that he didn't know "shorter", and he seemed even more doubtful about applying this term to a piece of wood.

Terry used the word "millions" as often as he could. Saying it obviously gave him great satisfaction. He sensed it was important in some way and no doubt he connected it with affluence. "Go on, have a candy, Miss. I've got millions." "There was a fire last night in our street and the fire-engines came. There were millions and millions of firefighters..." He also used it in more unusual ways. "Our Jean can stand up now, but I'm millions bigger than she is..." Not only did Terry need help with the meaning of words which were familiar to him, he needed to add equally exciting words to his vocabulary.

When children are stimulated to talk and then encouraged to do so freely, we are able to assess the quality of the words they use. If adults drown children in words and give them little opportunity to use words themselves, children will acquire a vocabulary with little conceptual foundation. The modern classroom is full of the sound of children's chatter, of children's questions, and of children thinking aloud. In such classrooms children are having every chance to become articulate adults with well-furnished minds.

9

The child's speech

Listening to speech is fascinating, for speech is eloquent of personality. Even when the words used are indecipherable, the tone of a speaker's voice and the way in which speech is used reveals much of his or her background. An imaginative listener can see the speaker's home, envisage situations and prognosticate about his or her reactions. When words are audible, even more is revealed. At every age a person is judged by speech, and speech is highly expressive of the person.

Children learn to speak between the time of birth and the age of two. The main part of the job has been done before they come to school. Speech demands of children not only the ability to vocalize and use words which mean something to them and to others, but also the necessity to put words together to form patterns which are socially acceptable. In speech, words are used as bricks and are carefully structured into artistic forms of communication.

Some of our children have acquired good speech forms before they enter school. Others will remain inarticulate through many of their primary years. The more inarticulate the child is, the greater is the need for expert help from an articulate adult. Unfortunately many of our inarticulate children attend schools where the adult child ratio is least favourable. The articulate parent often manages to place his or her child in a small class where talk between teacher and child is assured, but children of less favoured parents do not have such regular opportunities and so their first educational need is often skimped.

Many children are eager to use the speech they have when they come into school, and they will chatter incessantly if given the chance. Speech practice is as normal to them as breathing and moving. In a few cases the teacher's problem is in getting children to speak; more often the problem is in helping them to speak effectively and with greater purpose.

Although teachers have always recognized the need for the child to practice speech, it is only in recent years that the utmost need for that practice to be spontaneous has been recognized. Formal provision for speech in the form of object lessons, conversation, and verbal news periods are giving way to free interchange between child and child and between child and adult. It is not natural for young children to remain still and silent for long periods. The control of the class teacher is no longer judged by the ability to keep the children just where she or he wants them and silent until spoken to. Teachers hold the reins by guiding the children through their spontaneous chatter towards becoming articulate. The harmonious hum of a happy classroom suggests a control within which the child's individual modes of expression can flourish.

The spontaneous speech of children is stimulated in a variety of situations. It provides them with a means of getting to know other children. The content is not nearly so important as the act of exchanging words, so that speech forms a bridge between two people. If some situation such as mealtime provides a common interest, so much the better. Quite often, however, the speech of young children consists of a series of statements rather than conversation. Anita and Dave, both aged five, were sitting next to one another at the lunch table. They were eating ice cream.

> Anita: "My spoon's little."
> Dave: "Ice cream is best."
> Anita: "I can't get very much with a little spoon."
> Dave: "I can eat lots and lots of ice cream".
> Anita: "The spoon in the dish is better. I'm using that."

Two children may share an activity and appear to be exchanging their views. A careful listener will discover that their exchanges have little to do with the activity they share. Jimmy and Ron, aged seven, were constructing a lighthouse. Their problem appeared to be how to make the light-holder stay in place. Their fingers exchanged suggestions about strips of tape and various adhesives. What they were actually talking about was the hockey game they had witnessed with their respective fathers on the previous Saturday.

A highly educative use of speech is that which arises from the need to tell someone about an exciting experience. School offers the child particularly good opportunities in this direction. Each morning children burst into the classroom, scarcely able to wait to pour out their experiences to the teacher, who listens with more patience than parents often have time for. They have here the chance also to tell a whole group of listeners. School is full of exciting things to do and speech is a ready vehicle for expressing personal reactions to these experiences. The skilful teacher uses this expressive form of speech as the material for creative writing and reading (see Chapter 18).

When life is exciting and full of curious things, questions arise in the mind of a child. Here again a school is very well equipped with mature adult minds and informative books. The questions from children pour freely and teachers recognize in them highly effective opportunities for learning. The questions the child asks spontaneously are far more important than those asked by the teacher. They do, in fact, indicate the quality of provision made in the environment. If the teacher's material is sound and appropriate, it will provoke questions which lead to learning that is vital and relevant to the individual child.

Verbal reasoning is also often evident in the spontaneous speech of the child. Peter, aged six, crouching on the pavement, peered intently at the cracks between the flagstones. "They're going in and out and there's millions of them. They're ants. My Dad said they're ants. There must be lots of them down there. They make tunnels, like on TV. It must be all tunnels with ants rushing up and down under here. Perhaps they talk like people, not like ants. When they make tunnels, or they want to know which way to go, they must talk. I don't want to be an ant and live under there with people walking on top of me..."

Sometimes when children talk to themselves they are thinking aloud. Sometimes they are talking for the sheer delight of hearing the words. A small boy paraded the bank, while his father cashed a cheque, murmuring, "The Dukes of Hamilton and Porchester...The Dukes of Hamilton and Porchester...The Dukes of Hamilton and..."

The teacher, then, has little difficulty in encouraging the normal child to practise speech. The average four-to-five year old will say approximately 2 000 words per day. The teacher has an important part to play both in what children talk about and how they say it. The articulate person has something of interest to say and is able to say it so that he or she is understood. However capable of saying words children are, their speech is of little interest either to themselves or to others unless it is founded on a wealth of interesting things that they can do. Teachers and parents are responsible for furnishing the young child's mind, so that the ideas behind the words are rich and vivid. What children think and talk about depends on what they see and feel and hear. This is the fundamental reason behind the present-day classroom, alive with objects calculated to stimulate and extend curiosity and excite interest. Sometimes the uninitiated onlooker finds it difficult to link the child's play amongst these objects with learning which takes place in the mind, but it is in concrete surroundings that the contents of a child's mind first form.

During the first years in school children need a great deal of help with their modes of speech. We are more concerned with helping children to make themselves understood and with the quality of voice they use than in instilling rules for grammatical speech. Correct speech is very much a matter of taste and fashion. "Speech is how people speak, not how some authority thinks they ought to speak" (Plowden, para. 611). A person could memorize all the rules of grammar and still be inarticulate.

Children will convey their meaning if they understand what they are talking about and if their pronunciation is clear and accurate. Many of our children suffer from lazy speech or from imitating poor speech patterns. The best possible help a teacher can give is the good, clear, natural example of his or her own speech and the encouragement to express ideas as precisely as possible. "You know. It was a thingumy" does not describe the insect Kate found under the stones on the garden path. With help from the teacher she can do better.

Teachers have for many years sensed the usefulness of drama as an aid to good speech and mastery of the mother tongue. We have seen how the speech of the very young children is associated with their movement. The babbling of the baby enjoying the satisfaction of waving arms and legs about, the squeals, shouts and words which accompany early crawling, running, eating and dressing are evidence of the link between doing and speech.

As children grow older they will think aloud as they play. Ian, aged three and a a half, playing with his wooden engine, accompanied each action with words. "I'm going to put some coal in here and then you'll steam...Now we're ready and we're going a long way..." This association of words and movement is quite natural to the child, and in drama we see the synthesis of speech, gesture and movement.

Formal drama has no place in the primary school. A repetition of prescribed actions, accompanied by words which are put into the mouth of children , do little for them either linguistically or emotionally. The free dramatic play of children is a very different matter. Children are often liberated in speech through their own make-believe. Their passive vocabulary becomes active as their thoughts and feelings take the shape of words.

Simple equipment in the playhouse, a few drapes and simple furniture, will fire the child's imagination. They will become mother or father, the police officer, the doctor, the astronaut, or the teacher. Their imaginations create the scene and their minds find words to clothe their imaginations. In free dramatic play we see the preliminary practice of speech which precedes reading, writing, reasoning and understanding. At the same time children are learning to put themselves into the shoes of another person, which helps speech to develop from the egocentric speech of babyhood into the socialized speech of the adult.

Time spent in helping the child to develop powers of speech will provide us with an excellent means of discovering and liberating the child's personality.

10

Words in use

In school words are used in many ways. They are used, mainly by the teacher, for instruction. They are used for asking questions and providing answers. They are used as a means of expressing oneself, often with the hope of conveying meaning but sometimes as a form of verbal gesture as in "Oh no", "Good!", "Ah!", "Oh dear!" They are frequently used to report, record and describe. Sometimes they are used purely for pleasure.

Where the education of the young child is concerned, the emphasis is on the spoken uses of words. As the child matures, the many uses of words on paper play an equally important role. Even in higher and further education, we try to keep a balance between the spoken and written word in its various forms.

At one time it was the teacher who did most of the talking and much of what was said took the form of instruction and questions. Changing ideas as to the educator's role and the relative function of instruction in the learning situation have resulted in a change in emphasis. Today, it is the child who is encouraged to do most of the talking and it is more often they who ask the questions.

On entering school children are perhaps more used to instruction as a speech form used by older people towards them than any other form. During their early days in school children expect the teacher to initiate speech between them and a few simple instructions on the teacher's part help to make the child feel at home. The teacher tells the children what to do with their coats, which box they can regard as their own, where they can find paints, and so on. The teacher also shows where they fit in and gives them the feeling that they belong. Educators soon know by the way children interpret instructions something about their intellect and personality.

Once children have learned how to frame questions, they have the most effective means of assuaging their insatiable curiosity. If school provides an interesting environment, children will ask endless questions to extend or confirm their discoveries. The teacher's job is not always to provide an immediate answer. The spirit of enquiry can be maintained by providing further material which will lead the child towards finding his or her own answers. While helping the child to find answers from books or to explore further, the teacher keeps the situation alive. Answers given too readily are limiting and may terminate thought by terminating curiosity and enquiry. The teacher's answer sometimes takes the form of another question.

While the bulk of the child's questions are about things and facts, some are about life and living together. These are questions they cannot answer through further exploration of objects and materials. They are the most difficult questions of all for the adult to answer, for in answering we have no body of knowledge to refer to , but depend on personal opinion, which is emotionally biased.

When a child asks a question we know that he already understands something of the nature of the problem, for otherwise he wouldn't know what to ask. When Derek asks, "Are you nearly dead now you're old, Grandma?", he has recognized the connection between age and death. It's no use trying to evade the question by telling him not to be rude or that he isn't old enough to understand. He needs a simple and sincere reply, otherwise old age may seem to hold something sinister. On the other hand he does not need a long and involved analysis of the relationship between old age and death. His precise question should be answered as accurately and concisely as possible and at his own level of understanding. Sometimes by turning the question back on the child we discover how much he understands. A question may sound profound when in fact it is quite elementary. The enquiry, "What will happen to pussy now she's dead?" may require the answer, "We shall bury her", rather than involved explanations of pussy's chance of eternity.

A child may ask such a question at intervals as he matures. Each occasion represents a stage in his understanding and he can progress in this way towards full knowledge.

The visitor to the primary classroom is invariably asked, "Who are you?", or "Are you the inspector?" or "What is your name?" The child needs to identify, by naming the unfamiliar. This is particularly important when the unknown

45

is a person. By naming the person, fear of that person is removed. The child will need to know, too, "Where do you come from?", "Have you a husband?", et cetera. The new person has to be fitted into the child's plan of the world. This is part of the child's attempt to reduce the environment to something he or she can understand.

As children learn to master their mother tongue, they find in words a medium through which they can express what they feel and think. Being able to express what they feel helps them to understand and come to terms with these feelings. It is also a means of conveying feelings to others. The use of speech may come to replace aggressive action. Once a child can tell a teacher that he "wants a tractor like John's, but he can't because his Mom's got no money", he doesn't need to grab John's tractor as he plays with it and try to smash it up. Talking about his feelings instead of showing them in action applies to positive as well as negative emotions. The child who can tell her teacher she likes her will soon resist the temptation to fling her arms around her skirt every time she sees her. Her social behaviour matures as she acquires the ability to convey her impressions to others.

Children's expressive use of words is fostered in school. We give them much to talk about, to provoke feeling. We then help them to translate their experiences into words in such a way that they are understood and shared by other people. Children's recording takes a number of forms, such as picture-making, modelling, drama and movement. Recording in words is at first wholly in the form of speech. Only when children are fully articulate do we expect them to record on paper. There is no purpose at all in children copying what the teacher has written until they are able to tell him or her what to write down. We shall not speed the process of writing creatively by expecting children to copy words representing ideas and expressions which originated in the mind of another person. Too often children are turned against record-making because they are expected to record on paper with words when verbal recording is as much as they can manage.

Two boys were experimenting with water. With the aid of a nail and a hammer they pierced holes in the base of equal sized tins, one hole in the first tin and two in the second. They filled both tins with water and counted slowly as they emptied. One tin emptied on the twenty-ninth count, the second ran on until they had counted fifty-five. They described the situation as : "If the tin has two holes , it empties in twenty-nine, but if it has only one hole, it takes fifty-five". Their teacher, overhearing this suggested: "You can write about your experiment in our Discovery Book. I'll help you to say it properly." She spent ten patient minutes with the two boys, bending their description to an acceptable form which she wrote down for them to copy. They struggled for the rest of the morning and eventually earned the approval of their teacher. They avoided the water experiments for the rest of the week.

In another situation, a boy and a girl were making similar experiments. This time holes were pierced down the sides of a tin. There was great excitement when the tin was filled and allowed to empty. "It spurts right out. It's more at the bottom. When the tins get nearly empty the spurts get little." Their teacher joined them in their discussion. "What happened?" She encouraged them to describe in greater detail, helping them here and there with a more appropriate word and introducing the term "jet". She then reminded them of an earlier experiment. "Do you remember how you syphoned water out of the bucket? You could syphon water from this bucket into the tin and keep it full for quite a long time." Their experiments continued and their vocabulary increased to include the terms "water pressure" and "adjust". Verbal recording was far more appropriate than written or even pictorial recording at this stage.

Children's earliest utterances are a pleasure to them. Babies babble for the sheer delight of hearing themselves and for the rhythmic satisfaction babbling brings them. At all stages feeling permeates the child's use of words. Repetition adds a sense of security to this pleasure. Many nursery rhymes and jingles owe their popularity to the child's instinctive love of sound and rhythm. "Pat-a-cake, pat-a-cake..." is a favourite in most homes. (The child's rhythmic use of words is explored more fully in *Senses and Sensitivity* in this series.)

This love and delight in the use of words should be retained throughout life. It is far more important to enjoy one's mother tongue than to memorize patterns of printed words or to obey all the rules of grammar. A child of six will acquire words such as hippopotamus, elephant, supersonic, transfusion, evaporation, simply because he enjoys the rhythmic sound of them. They have magic and he will master them when words like to, at, in, bad, sad leave him unmoved.

Mastery of words makes them the child's playthings, and the seven-to eight-year-old will revel in puns and riddles, nonsense rhymes and jingles, secret codes and name calling, slang and foreign words, swearing and forbidden words. She will also appreciate the poetic use of words.

By the time the child leaves the primary grades she should be handling words with confidence and know enough about them to be able to play with them and use them imaginatively. This playing with words is the exploratory aspect of her learning about them. She must be given time to accomplish this exploratory stage thoroughly before hastening on to form uses of words. Words need never become a worry to the child, and the adults in the child's life are responsible for sustaining her delight in them.

11

The importance of literacy

Human beings are justifiably proud of their ability to use words. We alone use language. While all but the simplest animals have developed elementary forms of communications, only humans employ conventionalized gestures and sounds. From time to time we come across some higher form of animal life, such as the chimpanzee, the dog, or even the parrot, which has been taught by use to "say" words. These words signify little to the animal and cannot be used by it to communicate with a fellow animal. Only we use sounds and gestures which convey a verbal message. Only humans by walking upright, have liberated their hands and so can use language in written form.

Our words, then distinguish us from other forms of life. Through our use of words we can rise to abstract thought and so can live at levels quite unknown to animals. It follows naturally that our verbal accomplishment is a measure of our capacity to make successful adjustments to the world.

"Personal and social adequacy depend on being articulate, on having the words and language structures with which to think, to communicate what is thought and to understand what is heard or read".

One of our main functions as a teacher or parent is to help children to build up a varied and meaningful vocabulary and to help them to use words with skill and artistry. When we are dealing with young children we realize that their words are very intimately woven into their personal growth and that they are not yet ready to separate out the study of words from other aspects of their learning. Language is a pattern of habits rooted deeply in the child's personality, and what the child does with language in school needs to be built into the total language pattern.

As we have seen, in our society the child's environment is permeated by language. Everything they do demands of them that they shall use language. They meet their words embodied in all their experiences. When we try to help them to develop the use of their words we need to remember that words are part of what they are doing, a link in a sequence of activities and not something they can deal with in isolation. The philosopher may be able to contemplate the significance of the word "good", but children will only understand it in connection with themselves or things they like.

Our ultimate aim for children is that they shall be able to initiate communication by expressing themselves in spoken and written speech, that they shall be able to complete the communication by understanding the spoken and written speech of others, and that they shall love and enjoy words, and appreciate the appeal of literature.

In Western cultures a very high value is set on reading ability. Much of what children learn in school depends on their ability to deal with printed words. In some societies children would be taught to protect themselves and hunt as an introduction to adult life. In our country teachers and parents see reading as the key to learning. Sometimes, indeed, they seem to become obsessed by the business of teaching the child to read.

In the fifteenth century the invention in Europe of printing by movable type revolutionized the reproduction of literary matter. This event is responsible for the importance of print in our lives today, and the behaviour of teachers and children in school is profoundly affected by the printed word. On occasions we even lose sight of what printed words stand for; they seem to assume intrinsic value and dominate the purpose and life of the school. When this happens the joyful discovery of words turns to drudgery, and we have only ourselves to blame if the results are disappointing.

Because of our recognition of the importance and power of words, intellectual capacity and educational performance are assessed through linguistic skill. Children whose speech is poor and whose understanding of words is shallow find the recognition of words in print a very great problem, and much of what they are expected to do in the way of learning in school is barred them. As they proceed to the junior grades they find they can make little use of what school offers. Their intellectual rating becomes progressively lower than it should be.

Tests of intelligence are verbally based. They take the

form of spoken or printed questions and problems which require verbal responses. Even the non-verbal type of intelligence test depends considerably on the child's ability to reason by talking to herself or by using words internally.

These pressures have had a disastrous effect on the life of the schools. Linguistic accomplishment has become an end in itself rather than the natural product of experience. Once this happens, the use of words in a particular way, as in the case of reading or writing, gets out of perspective. Some teachers and parents are satisfied if a child can articulate words from a printed book and make the shape of them accurately on paper. The true purpose and use of words become lost in the empty pursuit of such limited skills, and the effects of education are assessed more and more exclusively by verbal examination.

Few topics of discussion create a more emotional response amongst literate adults than the teaching of reading. No doubt many adults today learned to associate their early reading stages with emotional situations, not all of which were very pleasant. We must avoid imposing on our children the dreary and disturbing experiences we were exposed to as children.

Many people firmly believe that the primary classroom should turn out accomplished readers, forgetting that learning to read is a prolonged and slow development which need not worry any child who has learned to speak and who is physically equipped to discriminate between visual patterns. The actual recognition of printed words is part of a process which started at birth and will continue until the day of death. At each stage in a child's school life they need help with the reading process. Students entering college often find they need a great deal of help when they are faced with unfamiliar material and unexpected extensions to their vocabulary. The unfortunate idea that reading happens once and for all in the primary classroom has created a great deal of misunderstanding about the school's true function. Teachers under unnatural pressure are filled with anxiety which conveys itself to their pupils.

From time to time depressing reports about the standard of reading in this country appear in the news. These reports seem to receive more attention than investigations which make it clear that the standard of education as a whole has been going up steadily since World War II. Some researchers seem to delight in discovering and exposing poor reading skill, and this kind of publicity can have a very detrimental effect on the teachers of young children. It takes confidence and conviction to resist these pressures and protect the right of children to develop not only in verbal skill but in all aspects of their personalities.

Junior classrooms and secondary schools must understand the part they play in the reading process. Many children need help all the way and most need help at some time or other, even after they have grown up. The help of a friend with an income tax form is frequently sought by quite intelligent adults. Learning to read is not a feat accomplished once and for all time. It is not a circus trick or a status symbol. It is part of the total development of the child's understanding of a literate society. When we recognize this fully, we shall be in a position to deal with the job of helping children to accomplish reading far more effectively than we do at present. If we have faith in children's ability to learn to speak, why can't we extend some of that faith to their ability to grow into the use of the visible extension of speech — the printed word? It is lack of faith on the part of the adult which creates some of the problems associated with learning to read. A child beset by anxious parents and teachers, who make words a nightmare for him is not likely to read with ease and delight. If he is ultimately condemned as being slow, whose is the fault?

12

The child's home background

The child learns to speak at home, and the family will play an important part in the development of language for the greater part of his or her childhood. As the child's circle of acquaintances and experiences widens, many influences will impinge on his speech. The confidence of success or the anxiety of a difficult job or the warmth of feeling excited by a romantic relationship will add qualities to his voice and words to his vocabulary. A fresh human situation, such as a university education or the dialect used by colleagues in an unfamiliar town, can influence his speech forcefully. He may even acquire a veneer of speech in contrast to his native tongue, but the underlying structure of his speech will remain and may even take him by surprise in a relaxed moment. The speech a person learns during his early, highly impressionable years will remain the foundation of his speaking for the rest of his life. The quality of the child's early linguistic environment will remain the most important factor affecting his linguistic development.

Children from different backgrounds have different opportunities for learning speech and this affects later learning. Interest in the study of social class differences in language and thought has intensified in recent years as a result of the work of investigators such as Bernstein with English children and Jensen with American children. Their findings suggest that disadvantaged children are most severely handicapped by poor speech and underdeveloped thought-processes. In our educational system, which is primarily designed to cater for middle-class children, the children from disadvantaged homes fail dismally and possible sources of intelligence remain undeveloped.

Steve, aged seven, had been absent from school. On his return, conversation with his teacher went like this.

Teacher:	"I missed you yesterday, Steven. Where were you?"
Steve:	"I were sick"
Teacher:	"Where were you sick"
Steve:	"On't sofa."
Teacher:	"I mean where on your body were you sick?"
Steve:	"Gota pain in my ear hold" (i.e. ear-ache)

Contrast this with Colin in similar circumstances.

Teacher:	"Hello, Colin. Where were you yesterday?
Colin:	" I woke up feeling sick, with a pain in my head. My mother took my temperature and it was 104."
Teacher:	"Did you see the doctor?"
Colin:	"Mother said she might call him, but Gran said, 'Oh, boys are up and down like yo-yos. I should give him a glass of ginger ale and keep him quiet' ".
Teacher:	"And did that work?"
Colin:	"Yes. You see, I ate too much ice-cream. There's a lot of fat in ice-cream and the ginger ale helped me to digest it."

Colin had his mother to himself for the first four years of his life. She talked to him and sang to him. Her voice was pleasing and Colin listened with great delight. She encouraged him in his vocal play and rewarded his efforts with her warm approval. She surrounded him with a wealth of happy experiences and a variety of play materials, and then provided him with good examples of speech with which to communicate his responses. Vocal interplay between himself and an attentive mother was the foundation of Colin's speech game. As he mastered his words, conversation with her helped him to acquire flexible modes of expression. Even when he was ill, she took the trouble to explain what she was doing with a thermometer and why she gave him ginger ale.

Steve competed for his mother's attention with two younger children. Older brothers and sisters looked after him as often as his mother did. He had no chance to develop a speech relationship with one person. Conversation in his home barely existed. If he was a nuisance he was cuffed or someone screamed "Stop your noise!" He learned to scream, too, because it was difficult to be heard against the background of perpetual noise from television, reinforced by the persistent clatter of life in a cluttered home. He didn't learn to speak well because he couldn't be heard and no one listened to him.

Many of our children come from homes where sentences are rarely spoken. Communication takes the form of grunts and gestures. A few words may be strung together without form or finish. They may be eked out by the repetition of "You know", "Like", "Because", et cetera. Information is incompletely conveyed. Ideas are disjointed. There are a few stock phrases from which the speaker selects one which seems to fit the situation. Speech is ugly and inadequate. In fact the only place in the home where articulate speech is heard is on the television. Much of this passes over the heads of the listeners because they lack the experience to provide the words with meaning. Books are rare and reading reduced to packages.

School must help children like Steve to develop his speech if he is to have a normal tool for learning. This is not, however, the only handicap which faces such a child. The disadvantaged home fosters other conditions which hinder the learning process in school. In the clutter of Steve's home there is no privacy. Clothing is common property and each morning Steve dons an assortment of garments from the pile on the bedroom floor. There is no corner in the house he can call his own, nowhere to hide a present for Mom or a treasured possession, no place where he can be apart from all the others. Even the intimate life of his parents is thrust upon him before he is old enough to understand. Steve as an individual scarcely exists.

On entering school, Steve's greatest delight was to be given a chair he could call his own. Only those who earn in the home are entitled to a chair. With ten to feed at mealtimes, standing around the table is the only possible solution. Without good washing facilities, keeping clean in body and clothing is a problem and Steve's Mom thinks twice before she changes his shirt. Steve is socially handicapped, and the speech of other children is not readily available to help him with his own.

In homes like Steve's, living is a perpetual battle. There is no harmony in the home and tempers are short. A father who drinks as a means of escape may get into financial trouble. He may even land in prison. Steve's emotional background is insecure. How can his teacher help him to express his experiences when they are ones he'd rather forget? How does he encourage him to recognize printed words when the emotional state of his mother has left him pathetically disintegrated? His teacher may make material provision to supplement his meagre experiences at home, but there is often little she can do to compensate for his arid emotional life. What conceptual foundation has Steve for the words his teacher can offer him? How is she going to fill in all the background to the words he will meet in books. Even the words of a first reader are outside his experience. Physically he could say them, but mentally he cannot recognize them at all.

In school Steve may ultimately learn a second language. This will not in itself make learning easier for him. During his early years he has learned to respond and think through gestures and actions rather than through organized groups of words. He was taught to obey by commands, reinforced by physical action if necessary, rather than by reasoning: by "Don't touch!" rather than by "The teapot is hot and it's too heavy for you to lift. You might spill the hot tea if you try, and hot things can burn." Language experience which steadily develops the linguistic skill of Colin would be unfamiliar to Steve. His teacher may be expecting him not merely to develop his use of language but to change his most deeply ingrained habits of thinking.

Linguistic change for a child tends to alienate him from his home background. His newly acquired language may not be socially acceptable at home. Either he must struggle with two different modes of expression and thought, or he must face the conflict of "learning to speak above his station". In underprivileged homes parents naturally feel an implied criticism if the speech they gave the child is not accepted in school.

What happens too often is that in school the child is taught to memorize word patterns by mechanical methods. Because the words mean little, what they convey means still less and is readily forgotten. Eleven-year-old Ivy went to private school from a one-room school in a small town. She was an intelligent child and she struggled valiantly to keep pace with her work. She confessed to another newcomer: "It's all strange to me here. I don't know what the teachers are talking about half the time." Her intellect remained untapped and she withdrew at the end of her first year, because she was unable to learn.

Young children's exploration depends initially on their own muscular activity. Intelligent babies may perfect the early stages of exploration on their own, but their discoveries can only become internalized with the use of language. However intelligent the baby may be, he or she depends on other people for the opportunity to learn language. He will only acquire the skill of words with the active help of another speaker. The child reared in a well-endowed home and attended by a communicative parent is given the best possible opportunity for developing speech and for exploring thought. The child brought up in the confusion of a disadvantaged home may make intelligent attempts to talk which either go unrecognized or else are ignored.

When such children come into school, because they are inarticulate they may be misunderstood, even written off as slower learners. They will need a teacher who is sensitive to their mental and emotional state. They will need an abundance of sensory experiences and concrete situations to enlarge their conceptual understanding. They will need a one-to-one relationship with a person whose speech is mature. Above all they will need time to mature in speech and communication before they can benefit from more abstract forms of verbal learning.

The best possible remedy, perhaps, for inadequate early speech experience in the home is carefully planned preschool education. Time, money and effort spent on educating the adolescent is wasted if the foundations are frail, and money spent on nursery school education would give a profitable return to the nation in increased intelligence.

13

How children meet words in their environment

In every aspect of daily life words are brought to children's attention. They use them in speech and hear them spoken by others. They see them used as labels on chocolate wrappers and cereal packages, on streets, buses and shops. Words give them directions such as up and down, in and out, hot and cold. They come to them in the form of stories to enjoy, as letters describing what is happening far away, and as news from all over the world. Children use words on the telephone, they collect words about their discoveries, they form an essential part of their dramatic play. They hear their own words on the tape recorder. They find out about the people with whom they live as often by using words as in any other way, and they learn much about themselves through the words of others. They use words to shape and convey their thoughts and feelings. Through words they learn how to reason. Radio and television, records and books bring words to them from the minds of other people. Life at home and at school is permeated by words. In short, they are the life-blood of learning.

In school, life revolves round what teachers say. Words spoken by them will have a most profound influence on what children do, how they do it and what they gain from doing it. Through their words children will learn about their own culture, its rules and attitudes, its aims and ideals. They will be shown how to behave in a group. What teachers say to them will be eloquent of their own personality and characteristic of the society they represent.

Teachers' speech and voice are their most powerful instruments, and the speech they use out of school will influence their speech in it. In fact everything they experience will influence their speech, because their voice in such an intimate part of their personality. Rough language, swearing, shouting and bawling can coarsen the voice. Even in schools where children learn mainly through their own activity, each child is subject to the sound of the teacher's voice in a large part of the day. They deserve good speech and a well-modulated voice. Teachers are apt to accept the quality of their own voice without question, forgetting that conscious effort can do much to improve it. Speech training may help a little, but clear thinking and sincerity of thought are perhaps the most effective means of improving the tone and quality of the human voice.

One of the teacher's main jobs is to help children to build up and reinforce their vocabulary. We should encourage children to talk about what they are doing and so clarify their ideas. At the right moment we may provide them with a word which describes effectively what is happening. He may, for instance, stir sugar or salt in water until the water is clear. He will try to describe the process, using words he knows, saying, "The sugar is all gone away". If at that moment the adult supplies the word "dissolve" he sees that it fits. He understands the word because he can endow it with meaning. He recognizes it as appropriate because it crystallizes his experiences and thought. He can then use it as an accurate description of what he saw happening.

When children start to include a word in their vocabulary, we can assume that the word means something to them. They may have heard the word "friend" many times, but they will only start to use it at about the age of six when they have experienced the satisfaction of mutual exchange in a relationship. They will start to use words such as "honesty" or "truth" when social experiences have helped them to understand something of their moral implication. That they start to use a word does not mean that they understand the full range of its meaning. Here again, the teacher can extend their experience or link them with others. The teacher may remind them, for instance of the ways in which they used the words "real", "right", "fair", and so on.

Words as sounds should predominate at this stage in the child's learning. Far too often it is words as visual patterns on paper which tend to become all-important, sometimes at the expense of the spoken word. We have come a long way from the day when children only heard themselves speak when they answered a question put by the teacher or articulated words from a reader. Few classrooms are silent; spontaneous speech is encouraged. Yet we still find anxious teachers thrusting words in print to the notice of children who cannot speak clearly, let alone shape words into sentences. A child cannot read until she or he has words to read with, for meaning resides initially in the spoken word.

When we ask children to read, what are we expecting them to do? The pattern on paper is a symbol for a pattern of sound. The pattern of sound itself is only recognizable if it symbolizes a familiar experience. The printed word "bat" represents the spoken word "bat". Even when spoken it needs to be set in a sentence before we know whether it means an animal, a baseball bat or a blow. A small child may have no experience of any of these or may know only a baseball bat. We present them with a very complicated process indeed when we ask them to read. We can train children to make the appropriate sounds when we point to a printed word, but those sounds only become reading when they are attached to children's personal experiences and so mean something to them. The accumulation of experiences takes time, and even when words are acquired in speech, still more time is needed to fill out their meaning. Unless this time is allowed to children their reading will be very superficial or else will become mere articulation at parrot level.

Reading is only worthwhile when the words speak to us from the page. We recognize them because they remind us of an event or situation; they convey a message, conjure an image, start us thinking because they are interesting. They spark off a train of responses. They are not ends in themselves. Some teachers feel satisfied if children merely make the right sounds. If words are not illuminated by children's inner vision, they are useless to them and drill in articulating them is a waste of time. We might as well drill them into articulating Greek or Russian. If we try to teach word-recognition in a vacuum, we may very well end up with non-readers.

The most meaningful words to children are their own, those they have selected from all the words in the environment as being of interest and use to them. Some of these words they will have in common with other children. Words such as mother, father, house, bed, dinner, are normally adopted by all children. But children will also have a vocabulary arising from their individual environments. A child who comes into school from an urban family will have different words from the child whose parents are farm people. Both sets of words are equally good because they are functional and we should take children's home language in to account when preparing material for them.

When we help them to make their own reading material, through putting their spontaneous words on paper, we are fitting their use of the printed word into the pattern of their individual learning. Yet some teachers are guilty of introducing words in print which bear no relationship to the child's experiences, as the first step in recognizing printed words. For example:

The ram runs
Help!
The ram runs at the hen
Help!

What does the child from the urban home or indeed from a literate home in any locality, make of this?

That we need to add words to the child's vocabulary is true, but we add words in action before we present the symbols of those actions to the child.

We may plan to extend the child's use of adjectives. A child tells you that tissue paper is "soft like skin" and we know that he is ready to understand texture words. We set out opportunities for him to experience various surfaces...a piece of bark, a polished wooden bowl, a shell, a piece of rough stone. We encourage the child to handle these objects and talk about them. He feels the need for words which describe differences in these surfaces, and we give him the words rough and smooth to add to the words hard and soft he already knows. Later, when he meets such words in print they will be associated with the feelings he has experienced.

Likewise the child exploring the use of her body in movement feels her way through such words as "fast", "slow", "crawl", "stretch", "swirling and twirling". Her imagination is fired and the words are tinged with poetry.

When the child watches the behaviour of dry sand she learns something about "sift", "dredge", "drift", "pile" or "cascade", and using these words is part of her active relationship with them.

While the child is building with blocks, she will learn to associate such words as "cube', "cylinder" and "sphere" with what her hands and her eyes have taught her about the shape of her bricks.

It is through such activities in which words and experiences become inextricably interwoven that the child grows to find in language a most perfect tool for her learning.

14

Listening and speaking

Children's first experience of speech is listening to the speech of parents, and learning speech plays an essential part of their early life in the home. Although the quality of their speech varies considerably, all children accomplish much during the first five years of life. School will offer them many opportunities for extending their speech, largely through sharing "speech" experiences with others. Listening will continue to play a leading part in speech development.

Even children from the articulate home still need a great deal of help with words, in the form of speech, before they can be helped to use them in other ways. Unless children talk no one knows what kind of help they need and teachers in progressive primary schools find many ways of encouraging the child to talk. Children for much of the time move freely about the room and when they do sit down, as often as not they face one another. Learning is approached through doing, and the common interests the children find in their jobs provide topics for discussion with other children and with the teacher. There are many interesting experiments to make, and discoveries excite speech as a way of expressing these experiences to others. The whole atmosphere of the school fosters communication and much of this exchange takes the form of spoken words.

When children have something to say they need an audience. Other children may listen to them, sometimes they act as their own audience, but what they like best of all is an adult to talk to. The greatest help an adult can give children is to listen to them, letting them open up their mind and shape it through putting their ideas into words. The adult who listens is allowed to reach into the children's minds and feel their way around children's understanding. We know, by what they say, what interests the children, how they feel about things, and how far they are able to reason. Their speech is a good guide to their personality and intellectual capacity. How much more do we find out about children's thought-processes in handling number relationships by encouraging them to talk about them, than we do if we show them how to manipulate numbers mechanically on paper.

The main problem for us as teachers is the number of children we want to listen to. They need listening to one at a time. Ten minutes spent with one child may last him or her for a week, but most children need this kind of help daily, almost hourly.

The teacher's time can be eked out by students on teaching practice, by visitors to the school, or by ancillary helpers such as school secretaries and caretakers. Some fortunate teachers have assistants or classroom helpers. One school invited mothers to share the work of the teachers for a short time each day. The principal could regard her listening as the main part of her job in her capacity as leading teacher of the school. In many elementary schools the principal makes personal contact with each child in the school, every day, a primary concern. These principals do far more for the child's linguistic development in this way than they would by hearing slower readers labour over dull pages.

From time to time the listening adult joins in with the conversation and leads the child towards greater precision in their speech. Sometimes the child's speech is faulty. Defects may be due to a physical problem. Often poor speech is the result of bad speech habits such as slurring, unfinished words, and so on. Emotional problems may affect speech; stuttering and stammering, for instance, can be due to lack of confidence and are often the result of parental pressure. Speech errors and speech disorders reduce the child's chance of communicating effectively, and they should be remedied at the earliest possible moment. Many local authorities employ a skilled speech therapist who will advise and assist if children are referred. Poor pronunciation and inadequate speech can have severe effects on the development of the child's personality and progress in school. Responsible adults must get skilled help for such children if they are to use their opportunities to the full.

Children need to speak, but they need to listen as well. They learn to speak through listening, and listening is where language experience begins. Educating children to listen is as important as educating them to speak. How many of us, as adults, are really good listeners? The good listener can often offer more help to a person in trouble than any amount of do-gooding can. A good lecture is useless unless the listener can listen creatively.

How often do we misunderstand because our ears and our minds have let us down? How often do we miss completely some of the loveliest of sound experiences, because we hear without listening? We never learned how to listen and much in life passes us by.

Listening to stories plays an essential part in the life of the child and the pleasure of the story itself is not its only benefit. In a story, or in poetry, human experience is interpreted. The writer uses words with skill, economy and beauty, weaving his material into artistic form. Carefully chosen and well presented, stories and poetry have a powerful purpose in education.

Young children listening can explore situations which supplement or extend their own experiences. They can learn more about themselves or identify themselves with the hero who meets and solves familiar problems. They can find relief from emotional strain. They can wing away into the world of their imagination. Many stories convey to them the attitudes of their society and the cultural beliefs of the race they belong to. Words capture them and compel them to listen. They take them by the hand and lead them into the world of fresh delight, where meaning is conveyed by simile, metaphor and image.

Stories for the young child are often better told than read. If you have made the story your own, you can dispense with the barrier of a book between yourself and the child. You are free to watch the child's face as you tell the story. You know by the expression on the child's face where you need to enlarge the meaning or modify the narrative. You are sensitive to the child's reactions and can adjust your story accordingly. Between them, child and teacher create the story. The intimate peace of storytime depends on the teacher's sensitivity to the material and to their children. Choose the story as much because you love it as because you think it might interest the children. Prepare it with care and create the right atmosphere before you share the experience with your listeners.

In story or poetry, the rhythm and beauty of the words hold the child with their magic. Children retain much of what they hear and want to hear it repeated. They may memorize whole poems in this way. Rote learning of poetry for the sake of repeating it has little value, but a mind stored with poetic phrases or sentences will lead to the full appreciation of the artistic use of words. We encourage good listening by giving children things which are worth listening to, and in Chapter 19 the literary value of stories will receive our attention.

A modern aid in the classroom is the tape-recorder and many primary teachers find this a valuable aid to good speech. In one classroom the teacher first recorded the spontaneous speech of the children as they chatted in the playhouse or made fabric pictures and models together. They were unaware, until she played the tape to them, of her activity. They were delighted to hear themselves speak and wanted to know "how it worked". Once the children were thoroughly familiar with the equipment, their teacher recorded their speech in a number of ways – reading their own stories and poems, telling stories, describing experiences or experiments, and so on. She then recorded their early morning chatter of "news" items from home. One child, hearing her recorded version of a television, program, said critically, "It wasn't the same really" (i.e. her report was inaccurate).

The teacher also recorded a story composed and told by Roy, an articulate boy of seven, and accounts by other children of books they had read in the library corner. After playing these records back to the children, the teacher typed them out. She pasted the typescript of Roy's story in a book which he illustrated. The accounts of library books were also pasted into a "Book about our Books". In this way story books and book reviews became part of the class reading material. Such books which contained the children's own words were highly popular.

In another classroom was a boy of seven who showed little interest in reading. Eric's teacher encouraged Eric to tell him about the things he liked doing. He taped his responses, and when he heard himself speak Eric volunteered, "I can tell you a lot more". His teacher took some photographs of Eric which fitted what he told him. He then made a book using the photographs and a typescript of the tape-recording. He left the "Book about Eric" in a prominent position on his desk. Eric saw the book with a photograph of himself and his name on the front. His curiosity made him anxious to find out what was in the book and he pestered anyone who could help him. The book proved a breakthrough for his reading skill.

The telephone is an interesting piece of equipment to be found in most schools and the job of answering it is highly prized. In some schools children sign up on a schedule for telephone duty when the principal is out in the classrooms. An attractive book-corner, occupies the helper in between calls. Although the helper may only ask the caller to wait while he asks the principal, this experience helps to emphasize the importance of speech and gives rise to some interesting observations.

"The lady said she was in another school. How can I hear her all that far away?"

"The gentleman said I was a clever little boy. How did he know when he couldn't see me?"

"It was a lady. She sounded like somebody's Grandmother."

Intercoms have been installed in some schools, so that communication between classrooms is established. The speech of many children improves tremendously and inarticulate children are often surprisingly liberated through this impersonal medium.

In ways such as these children are made more aware of their own speech and of the need for accuracy and good pronunciation. They are encouraged to improve their speech through conscious effort. They learn to realize its function in communication and to see the link between spoken and written words.

Most children are accustomed to the speech of radio and television broadcasters. In some homes unfortunately such speech is ignored and becomes merely background noise. We can use this material most effectively by encouraging children to listen and watch with discrimination. We can know and discuss with them suitable programs, not only those specifically designed for children, but certain serials, magazine programs and documentaries which we know by their time of showing children are likely to watch. We may not approve of some of the programs, but we cannot avoid knowing that they have a powerful impact on children and we can turn them to good account by helping children to develop powers of discrimination.

The teacher's own speech and how he uses it interpenetrate every aspect of the child's linguistic development in school. It will influence the child incidentally throughout her relationship with them. Sometimes he gives her the benefit of his own experiences. Sometimes he reads to her from a book a story, a poem, or information which interests her. This reading to the child starts in the home, when mother or father reads a bedtime story from a new Christmas book. It should continue at least through the primary grades. "Reading to" is a link between talking and reading. It helps children to bridge the gap between the spoken words they hear and the pattern those words make on paper.

In the modern world mechanical sound is becoming a threat and we grow increasingly conscious of the need to reduce harsh sound to a minimum. Even musical sound, if it creates a permanent background as it can with television and radio in every home, is capable of reducing our sensitivity to the things we hear. It is becoming more and more a responsibility of the teacher to help children to retain and develop their sensitivity to sound, particularly to the sound of the human voice, and so to maintain their delight in the joy of listening.

15

Becoming familiar with words on paper

Printed words have been part of children's environment since they were born. Many children of three can recognize the name of their street, the place where the bus stops, the notice which says people can't smoke. The initial stages of learning to read are something children share with parents and others who love them: it is a happy and joyous experience.

The four-year-old gets the television guide so that father can find out when their favourite program will be on. He knows which record plays the Toy Symphony. He recognizes the difference between Rice Crispies and Cornflakes on the boxes which look alike. He can recognize the drug store even in a strange town. The letter from sister Jenny tells mother what Jenny is doing, even when she's away at college, and with mother's help he can sign his name at the bottom of the letter mother writes back. Helped by a sympathetic adult, he makes these discoveries daily.

How much each child knows about words on entering school depends on intellect, the physical ability to see and hear, the range and quality of their experience, and the interest and attitude in the home background. Some children of five can read and enjoy a story; some have no idea how to handle a book.

Sheila came from a professional home. On her first day in school she produced a Bible from her new book bag and offered to read from it. She turned to the Song of Solomon and read: "For, lo, the winter is passed, the rain is over and gone, the flowers appear on the earth, the time of the singing of birds is come and the voice of the turtle is heard in our land". She read it beautifully and with feeling for the words.

Janice lived in a new suburb. Her mother bought a

women's magazine every week. Janice knew the magazine told mother how to make a delicious chocolate cake. She couldn't read herself, but she understood the purpose of reading and soon started to ask "What does this say?"

Stephen came from an illiterate home, and books meant little to him. He went into the book-corner and tore up one of the new picture books.

Each of these children has different needs. In some cases curiosity about words and a desire to read them has not been stimulated by the home background. The teacher must first stimulate an interest in words and then develop that interest.

The provision of books of the right kind in both the home and the school is essential. Even then it is not enough. A child needs to know that adults themselves enjoy and respect books. Of course teachers love books, but they need to let the child see that they do, and the place given to books in the classroom is the first indication of this to the child.

Parents and teachers today have a wonderful selection of books at their disposal. Covers are attractive and introduce the child to the contents of the book but the reading matter inside is even more important and every book should be read by a parent or teacher before it is released to children.

Reading material should be related to the immediate experiences of children; it should be well illustrated with pictures of good quality; the print should be clear, and the vocabulary good and closely related to that of the child. The first books a child meets will colour his or her future attitude to books and reading.

In school some of these books will be displayed on racks or tables in a corner of the classroom. Small comfortable chairs, flowers on the table, and the feeling that this is a pleasant, peaceful place will encourage the child to go there and enjoy the experience.

In other parts of the room books will serve a different purpose. Where there are objects of interest on the investigation table or displays are made of natural materials or the work of an artist, appropriate reference books will be associated with each of the exhibitions. With the help of the teacher or a friend a child can then find answers to questions stimulated by the displays. Even if she is only told what it says in the book, as the teacher turns the pages she will associate meaning with printed words as he shares the book with her. Reading with the teacher is an excellent help to most children at some stage in the development of their reading skill.

Opportunities for social play in school encourage the development of speech. In school the child has many experiences which stir her into telling someone about them. The teacher gives her writing materials, paper, crayons and paint, so that she can express her thoughts and feelings on paper, either in the form of pictures or in words.

One teacher took a series of photographs of the children at work. She pasted these into a book and let the children chatter about them; then she wrote what they had said beneath the pictures, thus making their first reading book.

Children can cut out pictures from magazines and paste them into scrap books. The teacher can then write for each child the comments they make about their pictures, and they can copy the words beneath hers.

A schedule is required for taking turns at the sand table or painting-corner. The teacher can show the child how to write his own name, so that he can sign up for himself on the appropriate list.

In short, we should use every opportunity in the child's day-to-day living to help him or her to understand the value of reading. In this way we establish the right approach. A good attitude on the part of the child provides a fertile background for more systematic help, and very soon the teacher can link the spoken and written words in more definite ways.

A neatly printed notice for example, reminds the child where to hang her painting apron; her name is written above her cloakroom peg. John made a clay bowl and displayed it on the shelf reserved for children's work, and the teacher labelled it: "John made this bowl".

In dramatic play children will imitate the adult, and the teacher can help them make out bills, invitations to parties, and so on.

On one occasion a parcel of patchwork pieces was brought for the sewing-table, and five children selected choice pieces and pasted them into a book. With the aid of the teacher they wrote their impressions of these materials, e.g. "Silk is thin. I like feeling it. It is soft. It looks like the Spring Festival." As a result of investigation, a child may make herself a book. One day the teacher gave Janet a paper serviette for the playhouse printed with the French words for numbers. Janet asked the teacher to explain the words and was thrilled to discover that people in other countries write numbers in different ways. With the aid of reference books she compiled her own book on "The Way Other People Write Numbers". Most children also like to make books about themselves, their families and playmates.

In these ways and many others, the child is exploring the use of words in the routine of his daily life. During the process of imposing order on the world children feel the need to fit these printed symbols into the pattern. As their minds become more firmly structured they recognize the need to understand printed symbols as an important part of being able to understand their environment.

In the early stages understanding is intuitive, and for some children intuitive thinking will make the symbols comprehensible. Most children, however, turn to the adult sooner or later for help in analyzing and interpreting them. It is at this point that we recognize the child as being ready to learn to read. Children's curiosity about visible symbols is aroused and their intense interest at this stage renders them highly teachable. This interest in symbols is not restricted to words in print. It extends to many other symbols on paper and the recognition of numbers, musical symbols, diagrams and maps grows alongside his reading. They are, in fact, part of learning to read.

The child may be sufficiently aware of the reading process to ask the adult: "Will you teach me to read?" Most children, however, are not capable of expressing their need so explicitly. They show us in other ways that they are ready and the sensitive parent or teacher can recognize the signs.

Children may ask: "What does this say?" They may reproduce isolated words amongst their scribble, or may point them out on a birthday card or in a book and ask for an explanation. Some will notice the initial sounds of words, or the recurrence of sounds as parts of words. Penny was interested in the illustrated dictionary in the reading-corner. She was delighted to find her own name beside the picture of a penny. She then pointed to other words on the same page in great excitement. "This starts like my name. That starts like my name.." She was told the sound "p" and spent the next half-hour finding all the words which included "p".

At first for the majority of children the single word is only part of a whole situation. It may act as a link in a chain of activity, e.g. "We must drive in through the right gate, Daddy. This is the one which says 'In'." Children will be interested in a complete page of reading if it tells them how the spider makes his web. Many children are unable for quite a long time to isolate separate words or to see differences between them. A child can of course be taught to recognize separate sounds and words, but he may not connect them with reading at all.

Most children, then, begin by reading simple sentences which have meaning, and only when the idea of reading itself is established do they analyze sentences into words. Beryl, at the age of four and a half, was devoted to her "Mother Goose Nursery Rhyme Book". At frequent intervals she would turn to "Old Mother Hubbard" and pester her older sister, "Let me read it to you". Her patient older sister would listen as Beryl burbled through the nursery rhyme, following the words generally with her finger.

One day she forgot her older sister. She stared at the page in great surprise and then, plucking each word separately from the page, read slowly: "Old...Mother...Hubbard..." Her excitement and delight sustained her right through the rhyme. The words had spoken to her from the page. They had revealed their secret. In a moment of insight she had accomplished the first major step in her interpretation of printed words.

For many children the process is slower, but it need never become laboured if we let them make their discoveries at their own pace and give them only the help they need. Over-helping will slow their pace, make them feel inadequate, deprive them of the joy of making their own discoveries, and even turn their joy into dislike and sometimes fear.

At a later stage, when reading ideas and attitudes are established, phonics may help children and they can use them as clues to solve their word problems. Some children "tumble" to an understanding of phonics and enjoy pointing out separate sounds within a word. But not all children find an analytical approach to word recognition helpful. Some teachers provide children with the whole word each time they are stuck until they become independent. Teachers who have helped hundreds of children through their early stages of reading would find it difficult to say precisely how they helped or how children bridged the gap between spoken and printed word. Most would agree that they surrounded the children with all they felt would help them offering different aids to individual children, and that in the end it was the children who accomplished the feat for themselves.

The adult who is sensitive to the needs of children as whole people, and who is tuned into the developing mind of the child, can give them a lot of help when they are learning to read. The emphasis must be on children's active learning rather than on teaching by instructing them. Some teachers feel guilty if the child has "learned to read alone". They don't feel they have earned their money unless they have "taught" him or her. Much of the systematic help we try to give the child is very misguided. Sometimes the child is hindered rather than helped by the material and methods we use.

The minds of active five- and six-year-olds are rich with words of their own. From various experiences they have acquired exciting words such as "speed", "crash", "blaze" "fire-engine", or lovely sounding words such as "stars", "darkness", "space", "Martians". They do not need two-dimensional paper pictures to illustrate these words for them. They are already illuminated by their own inner vision. The very saying of them lights their mind for these words are the material of their mind. They are the ones they are ready to recognize in printed form.

What do we do? Some teachers help children to meet these words in printed form by writing them down for them and helping them to write them themselves. These teachers may then type out the words so that they resemble the words in printed books. Many teachers, however, ignore these words completely. They present the child with a collection of words thought up by a person who has never met either the child or teacher, and then expect the child to be interested in them.

Because the words are unfamiliar they are illustrated by flat paper pictures, which often provide little clue to the meaning. The first stages of existing reading schemes, even those published by reputable firms, could scarcely be classified as good literature. Some are sheer gibberish and an insult to children. Children deserve material of literary value as their introduction to the printed word.

Most teachers would agree with these comments and would still persist in using readers. They seem to provide the teacher with a sense of security. They feel assured that they have done what they can when they have given the children their daily dose of a controlled vocabulary.

In some schools readers are introduced to the children as soon as they enter and teachers are preoccupied with hearing children "read" or practice the skill of word recognition even before the child knows what reading is about.

A teacher of children from professional homes once confessed: "I give each child a reader as soon as they come into school. They keep it in their box. When mother asks anxiously, 'Are you reading yet, dear?' the child can set her mind at rest and I can get on with the business of teaching him to read." Perhaps the main purpose of readers is to allay the anxiety of parents and teachers. In Chapter 17 we will consider the value of readers more closely.

There are four recognized methods of giving systematic help with word recognition. The alphabet method, by which children use letter names to spell out words, was used in many primary classrooms during the last century. This is virtually obsolete. In the phonic method, children are taught the sounds of letters or groups of letters as clues to recognizing words. Unfortunately the English language contains many words which cannot be deciphered in this way. Words which can be sounded phonetically make dull reading material: "the bad fox is sad" will scarcely interest a young child. In the "whole word" or "look and say" method children memorize the whole word. Any word of interest to the child can be used, but it provides no clues for unfamiliar words and children depend on the adult to tell them each word. The same principle applies to the sentence method, but here they are told the whole sentence. Reading material is based on the children's own experiences and this procedure helps them to read such sentences as "John will give out milk today".

Few teachers use one of these methods exclusively. Some use a combination and adjust the method to the type of child. Many teachers proceed to help the child without reference to particular methods at all; they simply offer such help as seems appropriate and encourage the child to learn as naturally as possible. They see the recognition of words as a stage in the structuring of the child's mind. Their approach is based on Piaget's view of child development. The view teachers hold of education is clearly reflected in the way they approach the teaching or learning of reading.

Once printed words are familiar most children find them interesting for their own sake. They enjoy playing with them, grouping them into families, seeing little words in big words, finding words which begin the same way and so on. They enjoy collecting words: colour words, doing words, words about water, words which sound lovely. In this way the use of dictionaries grows alongside creative writing. A child's dictionary book is simple at first – merely a plain book in which the teacher writes the word the children need for their writing. Later the words can be classified in groups or in alphabetical order. Clearly the development of writing and reading is inseparable, and children's command of words grows through their own use of them.

Learning to read is a continuous process. Except in a very few extremely abnormal cases all children can learn to read, but the pace must suit the child, and the junior and secondary grades must take the responsibility of continuing the teaching of reading. The child who gets there first is not necessarily the best reader, and many children who make no real start until they are seven or eight can rival the early starter at the age of ten. A person has seventy-odd years to devote to his reading. We can allow children five or six years of doing things which enrich words with meaning before we subject them to any form of direct tuition. Above all, the attitude of the adults who help children is far, far more important than the methods used to instruct them.

16

The joy of reading

Although books have existed since the fifteenth century, the practice of printing them for children is a comparatively recent development. The idea that children should enjoy books scarcely occurred to our ancestors and until the seventeenth century the only books printed for them were school textbooks and books of etiquette. Puritan writers such as John Bunyan and James Janeway, whose aim was to "rescue" children, were amongst the first to write for them, and Pilgrim's Progress appeared in 1675.

John Locke in the late seventeenth century thought children should learn to read and have suitable books from which to do so. He was concerned about the grave shortage of material for children. Adult books such as Defoe's *Robinson Crusoe* (1719) and Swift's *Gulliver's Travels* (1726) were to become popular with children, but it wasn't until the rise of the middle classes in the latter part of the eighteenth century that the idea of children's books became established. The first bookshop for children was opened by John Newbery in 1745.

Early books for children such as Samuel Richardson's *Pamela* were neither suitable nor attractive. The late eighteenth century found cheap books circulating amongst ordinary people who were then becoming literate. Most of these were of poor quality and have not lasted. Alphabet books were popular. Fairy tales were frowned upon; John Locke had thought them "perfectly useless trumpery". Nursery rhymes were acceptable, and family stories with a moral in each chapter, such as Martha Mary Butt's *History of the Fairchild Family*, were considered improving for children.

It wasn't until the nineteenth century that good writers were prepared to write for children. The population was becoming better educated and a breakthrough in children's literature included Lewis Carroll's *Alice in Wonderland*,

Charles Kingsley's *Water Babies*, and Louisa Alcott's *Little Women*. Before the First World War we find a first golden age of children's literature. Kipling's *Kim* (1901), Kenneth Grahame's *Wind in the Willows* (1908) and Barrie's *Peter Pan* (1906) were books which are still popular today.

The First World War affected children's literature through the loss of writers and through paper shortage. Quantities of books of poor quality followed the war; the few exceptions included A.A. Milne's *Winnie the Pooh* (1926), the William books of Richmal Crompton (1920s) and P.L. Travers's *Mary Poppins* (1930s)

The Second World War brought its restrictions, but today we have entered a second golden age. Children are recognized as prolific readers. Science fiction, school stories, novels, plays and poetry flood the market. Publishers employ every technique to make books attractive and educative. Children are encouraged to read by the books themselves. We are as concerned about the material we offer children as we are about the way we help them acquire the skill of reading. What they read is as important as how they read it.

Nowadays we expect every citizen to read. Literature of all kinds is available at prices which meet the pocket of the poorest person. We expect to find the printed word in many forms and books in every home. We regard the acquisition of reading as an essential skill.

The way we teach reading is often influenced by methods of instruction employed by our ancestors. A brief consideration of the development of these methods helps to explain the unfortunate attitude on the part of many parents and teachers when helping children today.

One of the earliest aids for children was the hornbook. This at first was a thin piece of horn and later a small piece of paper, fastened to a thin board. At the top of the paper the alphabet in capital and small letters appeared. Then came the vowels, double lines of ab, eb, ib, and so on, and the benediction. The Lord's Prayer or roman numerals occupied the remaining space.

The Primer was originally a book of private devotions: the Lord's Prayer, the Ten Commandments, and the Psalms. It was inexpensive and intended to help poor people to learn how to read their Bibles. The alphabet was frequently included. This is why elementary books for the use of children became known as primers.

People in the seventeenth century thought of the

Comenius
Pestalozzi

child's mind as a *tabula rasa,* on which patterns of learning were etched by instruction. The idea of the mind as a developing aspect of the person, which matured stage by stage into its adult structure, was considered by only a few people like Comenius and Pestalozzi. The significance of maturation was quite unthought of, and meaningless sounds and symbols were instilled in unformed minds in the hope that the child would learn to understand them by memorizing them. Picture alphabets and rhyming jingles were thought to be an introduction to reading, as in the following cases:

> "In Adam's fall   "Zaccheus he
> We sinned all."   Did climb the Tree
> "Heaven to find   Our Lord to see."
> The Bible mind."

Speaking of elementary school education in England, John Locke informs us that in 1690 "The method to adhere to is the ordinary road of the Hornbook Primer, Psalter, Testament and Bible; these are the only books used to engage the liking of children and tempt them to read".

There were three reading classes in the school. The beginners joined the Psalter class. The Testament class followed and the Bible class was the final goal. Children went through two chapters at each session. They had to spell out the words in the section read.

Spelling books became popular in 1750 and for seventy-five years they proved practically the only source of instruction for school children.

In more recent years help given to children in school has ranged from instruction of the whole class to individual help. Few schools would expect children to chant in unison as the teacher points out words on a blackboard, but one can still find schools where reading round the class is practised, and in many schools children in small ability groups are expected to read in turn. Sometimes silent reading takes place as a special exercise. Comprehension of the matter read may be tested.

In many primary classrooms teachers hear children read aloud individually. The material they read is as often from their own writing as from printed books. Teachers find assurance in hearing the child articulate the words and use this as a measure of the child's skill. Some schools have more confidence in making words a vital part of children's life and teachers assess children's skill by what they absorb rather than by their ability to recognize and articulate each word. Ultimately reading aloud is largely discarded and one wonders whether some children ever need to do it. There can be no greater delight for a teacher of young children than to find a child chuckling to himself over a book or lost in the world of a story he can read to himself, unless it be the child who, independent of his teacher's help, can satisfy his curiosity through information he collects from books. In whatever way we help the child to acquire reading skill, the end-product should always be silent and fluent.

Today we have at our disposal a wealth of material. Much of it is good, some of it excellent, but there is still a distressing amount of trash amongst printed material for children. Gimmicky books, flashy jackets and covers which are little guide to the contents, and an indifferent or inaccurate text often tempt the adult to pay up. There is a tendency also to illustrate books so profusely that nothing is left to the child's imagination. Pictures should illuminate, not dominate. A good story will weave its own pictures in the mind of the reader. Some books, of course, depend more on picture than text to convey their message. Here again, pictures should be authentic in detail and well produced. Some products are an insult to children. The selection of books will be considered further in Chapter 17.

Only material of high quality is suitable for the young reader. Books should tempt children to explore and then satisfy their curiosity with their delight. Reading is an exploratory activity. It should be a joyful experience at all times. It can be shared with another person or it can be individual, but it should never be a form of drudgery. At all stages the attitude of adult and child to reading will colour the learning books offer.

Reading is an exploratory activity

17

The literary value of books available

The use adults make of words and the type of literature they appreciate depends on the words they have met and the ways they have seen them used. The words they first meet as a children remain their words for the rest of their lives. Many of our children meet words used well in print for virtually the first time when they enter school.

When we select material to put before children we must ask a number of questions. What do we look for in a book for children? What happens to books in schools? And, most important of all, are the words used the right ones?

Certain principles guide our selection of books of any kind for children. They should be well printed on paper of good quality. The print should be clear and large enough to suit the visual acuity of the age-group; illustrations should be authentic. Photographs are more informative than drawings and diagrams. They can be used to break up the text into digestible pieces. Whether the child can read or not, large slabs of unbroken text are discouraging.

Books make their first appeal to the eye. Colour is important, but we should not suppose that young children always like gaudy colours. The work of a good artist always appeals and crude bright colour which catches the adult eye is not necessarily the child's choice. Some children indeed prefer black-and-white etchings or charcoal designs. Not all children need to find stories profusely illustrated, for the story which is well written conjures its own pictures in the mind of the child. Poetry in particular should be sensitively illuminated. The mind of the children are alive with vivid pictures, and they do not need the imagination of others to bring stories to life for them.

While books need strong covers and should be reasonably durable, they should not be too much so. They should be used with respect because their quality is good, but they should be used to death and then replaced. We should never find in school either books preserved in their original splendour or books so dog-eared that they become distasteful.

A book should also appeal to the hands. The shape, size and weight of books are important factors. Giant, showy books persuade money from the pockets of adults, but children will love neat, well-designed books which will rest on their knee and sometimes the small book they can hold in their hands. Books with plastic or varnished pages may be strong, but they rarely appeal to children's fingers. On the other hand, a polythene jacket to protect an attractive book-cover heightens its attraction.

Very often parents and even teachers buy a book because the cover is promising. Every book should be read before it is purchased. Parents welcome the help of the teacher in selecting books for presents, and a school display of suitable books just before Christmas will guide parents into spending money wisely.

Most local authorities try to be generous with book allowances and the money is spent on a wide range of individual books rather than on sets of books. Children are learning to read from books which interest and inform. The skilful teacher can guide children towards finding what they need in books they can understand. Children may require help here and there with the words, but they accomplish the basic stages of learning to read by reading from good material.

We still find in many schools that readers are used to introduce children to words in print and then to give them practice in word recognition. The guarantee of a controlled vocabulary fed to the child in graded steps is the absolute antithesis of the true aims of reading. It may provide a sense of security for those teachers who believe that, if they take the child methodically through the stages prescribed, then the miracle of reading is assured.

Try reading aloud from cover to cover a beginning reader. Is this the way children speak? Is this material calculated to entice the children to try to master the skill which will help them to read more of it? Does it even make sense? How many of these early stages can compete with the wide range of attractive books available? The more advanced readers contain very good stories and deserve an honoured place in the book-corner, but too many of the books which are intended to serve as the children's introduction to reading are gibberish and more likely to put them off reading than to encourage them to go further.

Children have words of their own. When they hear the words they love their minds illuminate them with living pictures from their own experiences. Some words are common to all children, but each child has his or her own collection of words. It may be excavator, truck , and tractor which interest Alicia, and indigo, ruby, and paint which interest Chris. We should use the material in the children's own mind if we want them to read in the full meaningful sense of the word. Ways in which we can help children to read their own words will be discussed in the next chapter. Words from the mind of another person will interest them later, but to meet their own friendly words in another shape makes reading a natural development of their own speech, and this is what reading is.

Many children come into school from homes where books are scarce or non-existent. They need help in their use of books, and introducing children to books is the first step towards helping them to use them effectively. However well books are displayed and organized it is not fair to expose children to them unaided. They need to learn from the adult how to respect and handle them.

Teachers let the children see how they use books and how to care for them. For instance they may share the unpacking of new books with children singly or in small groups. "Here is a lovely new book. We're the first people to open it and look inside. What do you think it will be about? The little yellow duck is funny, isn't he? Shall we see what he has been doing?" By being introduced to a book in this way, the child is given some idea as to its contents before it goes into the book rack.

Teachers may read a story or perhaps a poem from a chosen book which is then left for the children to investigate. They may help a child to find an answer to her questions by sharing an informative book with her. They make books for the children or help them to make books themselves, and these, too, take their place amongst those purchased. A child who has made a book is aware of the care and effort needed to produce one. Attitudes of delight and respect are established in him right from the start.

Books should hold a prominent and honoured position in any school and in every classroom. Their position and the way they are arranged influence the use made of them by children and teachers. Books tightly packed behind glass doors with only their spines visible through the windows do not encourage anyone to explore them. Books isolated in a central part of the school may be sought after by older children, but young children need their books around them in the room while they work.

Books should be displayed with their covers showing. Racks made for this purpose can be purchased, but suitable display shelves can be improvised and need cost little. Wooden slats nailed to the back of a cupboard with curtain wire to support the books, plywood nailed to one side of a wooden horse, again with curtain wire to support the books, tables or shelves with metal slips to hold some books upright, peg-board with metal clips – all are ways of arranging books so that they can be seen and easily reached.

Often displays of materials are associated with appropriate reference books in which children can find out about the things which interest them. Books on a table in a corner screened off from the rest of the room encourage quiet reading. The books may carry some guiding mark which indicates the difficulty of the material. "L" for learner or "A" for advanced reader may help children to select a suitable book. Flowers and comfortable chairs add to the appeal of reading-corners. Some books may be displayed farther afield, in a peaceful corner of the school hall or in a spare classroom. Here children from all parts of the school can share books, often helping one another to read them. Children gain confidence they may take a book they are writing to complete it where the sources of information are available.

The use children are making of books in a school is a safe guide to their skill in reading. If children can find their own answers from books, if they can enjoy in private a good story or commit to mind the words of a poem, if they can record their discoveries and write their own stories, need we ask them to read aloud to us? Does it matter whether they can recognize each separate word in a book or whether they read all the words? Is it not the meaning behind the words they are after? Can we not let children enjoy books in their own way, helping them to decipher words when they need it? Need children plod and stumble, sound by sound, through what they read? Do they all need the same kind of help? We should not, it is true, forget the need for thorough reading, for extracting the full meaning from what is read, but doesn't this depend more on the appeal of the content than on the visual recognition of the words?

Tony was a quiet child of six. He stood patiently in the

teacher's small circle, listening to his friends as they read aloud in halting voices. When his turn came he sounded each word carefully and completed correctly the sentence he was expected to read. The group changed and Tony slipped his reader away on his shelf. He then retired to the book corner and was immediately caught up in the words of his favourite story book.

The teacher knew Tony could read. "But I have to make sure," she explained, "that he isn't missing any words out, or getting some of them wrong." Would that teacher read each word separately, or read every word of the novel she took to bed at the end of the day? How can we expect children to become good readers if we teach them to read with the brakes on?

A visitor to another primary class was asked by a child of five: "Do you want to see the principal? She's Ms. Digby and she's in the room with her name on the door. I've just seen her and she's given me this new book out of the box she's unpacking. It's all about a baby seal who lived in a nursery bed and had to learn how to swim. He had a white coat before he got his seal coat and I'm taking the book to my teacher for her to read it to me again."

In this school books lined the walls of the corridor. A group of children were gathered round a table in the foyer. They were comparing the moss against the stones in a shallow dish with pictures in a book. One child read from the book to the other children.

Classroom doors stood open. Inside each room children could be seen making scrapbooks and picture books, writing stories, making books about space travel, doll's clothing, and picnics in the park. One group was making jam tarts, following the recipe printed in a book. Some boys in a hall were following the instructions they had found in a book for making a water organ. One child stood in front of the piano fingering out a tune from the simple chart made by her teacher. Another child was absorbed in merely turning the pages of a book in the book-corner, because this was the stage she had reached.

Everywhere in the school books were an essential part of the child's life and of his learning. There was no doubt in the mind of the visitor as to the quality of learning taking place in a school such as this, where children had learned to live with books in their hands.

The aim of teaching reading is to make life richer and more meaningful. Sometimes teachers make oral reading skill their goal and select material with this aim in view. They decide what children shall read and how they shall read it. Then they wonder why these children are such poor readers when they reach secondary school.

If we select books with care and surround children with material of real literary worth, if we give them time to browse and to choose what interests them to read and if we help them to enjoy it we are fostering positive reading habits which provide the sound foundation of later literacy. What we do about books at this stage should encourage children to go on reading, and they will read if we make it worth their while to do so.

18

Imaginative writing

The words which children find most interesting are those which they have discovered themselves. Helping children to write their own words on paper shows them not only the purpose of creative writing but also helps them to understand the nature of reading. Reading and writing are two parts of a single process and develop side by side in a progressive primary classroom. Many children learn to read as much through their own writing as from printed books.

We all live in a world of talkers. The creative and imaginative use of words in the form of speech has developed in us naturally as part of our adjustment to an articulate society. If we can talk we have it in us to become writers and most of us employ a variety of forms of creative writing during the course of our daily lives. Letter writing is virtually universal, and as transport facilities increase so communication by written word plays an ever-increasing part in the affairs of human beings.

When writing to a friend most of us compose good letters, because we write in a relaxed relationship and enjoy telling our thoughts to a sympathetic person. We describe a new hat, we report an event, we express our views about pay negotiations, we tell a story about an experience. Each of these represents a form of creative writing. We have the ability to use words on paper but how many of us can weave those words into poetry, create a spell-binding story, or narrate a really vivid account of a situation? How many of us feel inhibited when it comes to the poetic and imaginative use of our own words? And, although most of us would enjoy the thrill of meeting our own words in print, we are often reluctant to admit to being the author of a poem.

The mind of the adult is rich with experience, but most of us feel inadequate when expressing ourselves on paper.

Somewhere along the line we could have been helped to translate the material in our minds into some really artistic form, but instead, what happened? The teacher said: "Be creative for twenty minutes starting now at half-past nine on Monday morning". We were given comprehension exercises or instructed to fill in the missing words. We had exercises in punctuation and grammar, and we were afraid to try new words in case we spelled them incorrectly; we didn't talk much about our words, and the right word constantly evaded us; we were given a stilted and inadequate handwriting style and our thoughts stumbled through physical frustration; finally, our painstaking efforts were scored with red pencil until we revolted against them. Our ultimate goal was to write answers to examination questions. We learned to cling to what was safe and would look neat and tidy, and imagination remained dormant and became stunted.

A child finds a toad in the garden. He notices its queer skin and its bulging eyes: he watches it leap. He must tell someone about it, and he'll talk to anyone who will listen – his parent, his teacher, his friend. If there is no one around he will talk to himself. He may try to draw or paint all he has experienced. This is his material for creative writing, and with some help he can put what he has to say on paper using the words he has spoken, and his experiences will be extended and preserved.

Some children come into school scarcely able to make recognizable shapes on paper, some even find difficulty in holding and using a pencil. Some children by the age of seven or eight are writing poetry and "novels" of about seven or eight hundred words. Helping the child to write spontaneously and independently of help from an adult is a magnificent feat of skill which many teachers accomplish. Most children will continue to require some assistance for many years after they leave the primary grades.

In order to write imaginatively children must have something to write about, a wealth of words with which to express their ideas, the tool of handwriting, the opportunity to write when they feel creative, and time to finish their work. These are the things which the teacher can provide.

Many children begin to write before they can read. Their childish scribble may include the odd letter or number symbol, or even whole words and parts of sentences. Sometimes children will tell the onlooker what their "writing" says, or alternatively they may ask to have it translated for them. At a very early age children are anxious to express themselves on paper, and their writing, picture-making and reading are part of this effort to communicate. They are very proud of the results of their efforts and will show them to an adult, hoping for approval. Their emotional satisfaction here is highly important in establishing their later attitude. Children who see their scribble consigned to the waste-paper basket may lose respect for their work and their enthusiasm will wilt.

David loved the new climbing apparatus. He got a plain paper book from the writing-corner and filled it with coloured pictures of himself using the apparatus. He chattered to his teacher about his pictures and she wrote a simple caption beneath each: "I like the ladder best", "I can swing from the long rope", and so on. David read the captions. He then went over them with his pencil. As he reached the end of the book, he copied the captions beneath his teacher's writing. He then wrote THE END independently.

Michael's favourite toy was his aunt's old typewriter. He typed messages and left them for parents and relatives to read. He could type words before he could write them and the typewriter was a tool he could use to help him transfer his thoughts to paper.

Sometimes the actual writing is done by the teacher as an extension of the child's speech. The child uses the teacher as a tool. Elizabeth loved poetry, and poetic ideas often sprang to her mind. At six she found handwriting difficult and made frequent use of her teacher, "I've got another story," she would exclaim, "Will you write it for me, Mr. Matthews... 'The rain drops, the silver drops on a spider's cobweb'". By the time she was seven her academic skill had caught up with imagination.

We can enrich children's vocabulary and stimulate their desire to write in a number of ways. We do it directly by introducing children to a wide variety of experiences which make them want to talk and, later, to record. This does not mean we must be constantly organizing ambitious expeditions. Children are just as excited about the beetle scurrying out of the crack in the pavement as they are about the elephant in the zoo.

Indirect stimulation comes from introducing children to the best that literature can offer. We choose stories that are told well, using good vocabulary. Our selection of poems includes as much "real" poetry as jingle or verse, for the work of the artist inspires and provides a good pattern. We cultivate in our children an appreciation of the beauty of words and the exquisite use of them. We want them to capture something of the magic and wonder evident in Eleanor Farjeon's poem *What is Poetry?*

> What is poetry? Who knows?
> Not the rose, but the scent of the rose;
> Not the sky, but the light of the sky;
> Not the fly, but the gleam of the fly;
> Not the sea, but the sound of the sea;
> Not myself, but what makes me
> See, hear and feel, something that prose
> Cannot; and what it is, who knows?

We encourage children to collect words - about light, for instance. The language of light is almost poetry:

> Ray, beam, gleam, moonbeam, dawn, aurora,
> Spark, flash, blaze, flame,
> Shine, glitter, twinkle, flare, shimmer,
> Scintillating, translucent,
> Transparent, limpid, glossy, iridescent

We have considered the importance of the teacher's own speech in helping children with their words. Many of our children come from homes where English is not the first language. The first good speech these children hear spoken personally to them may be that of their teacher. Because the teacher is such an important person to them they will take note of her speech and try to use it themselves. They will find that there are more widely understood ways of saying "summat" (something), "on t'road" (on the road), and that good speech is pleasing to the ear.

Their teacher will help them to use their words accurately and convey their meaning precisely. When they say that the sun has "sucked up" the water from the wet playground, she will give them the word "evaporate". She will encourage them to perceive with care, for accurate observation is conducive to good writing. What they touch they will learn to feel, what they hear they will learn to listen to and what they look at they will learn to watch. Then their mind will receive a rich store of information from which to weave their thoughts.

Writing materials should always be available in the classroom, and if they are attractive they will encourage the children to record their thoughts and feelings. There is some desire in humans which drives them to make their mark on a plain surface, and the teacher who provides an assortment of home-made books with coloured card covers will have as many candidates to use them as there are books.

Unlined paper will give children a surface free of restrictions when their attempts to write are immature and unformed. Thick pencils are easier to handle for the child whose finer muscles are undeveloped. Crayons for illustration, boxes of pictures, equipment for making small books quickly as they are needed – all are part of the writing-table.

In many schools children are taught script print as a preliminary to handwriting, but a number of schools have adopted a simple cursive style, such as that devised by Marion Richardson, as a suitable beginner's tool. This style has the advantage of being a natural development of children's early scribble, and by the time the children are seven and their ideas flow a cursive style enables them to set them down quickly and legibly. It is moreover, a style which provides the foundation for an adult hand; there is no switch from script print to handwriting on entering the junior grades. A cursive hand may take a little longer to acquire in the early stages but it provides children with an adequate tool by the time their thoughts are beginning to take shape.

Sometimes the craft of handwriting is taught as an art form not necessarily connected with what the child wishes to put down on paper. Marion Richardson recommended the teaching of her style through a pattern approach with a brush. Most schools help children to acquire their handwriting as part of the effort to express their ideas on paper. They are given the tools as they go along, but emphasis may be placed on the handwriting itself from time to time as, for instance, when they compile an anthology of "Poems We Love".

Much depends on the good model provided by the teacher. Children are faithful imitators and will take care to reproduce the teacher's characteristic style. Few schools nowadays expect children to fill copy books. Copying from the blackboard is also unusual. Indeed for the young child the problem of visualizing and then reproducing blackboard copy renders this a very difficult exercise. Copy beneath a good model, with some help for individual difficulties, is perhaps the most appropriate way to acquire the tool. Handwriting is only a means to an end, not an end in itself. The study of handwriting as an art-form can come later, if required.

When children first try to put down their thoughts on paper we expect immature standards in appearance, spelling and punctuation. Our first aim is to encourage free translation of ideas into written form. As their writing matures, children can understand the need for accuracy, legibility and punctuation, if what they have written is to be read by others.

In the very early stages the teacher provides children with a copy of what they want to say. Very soon the child will try to write some words without the aid of the teacher. Some children are very independent, and although they may write queer versions of the words they want to use it is advisable to encourage them in their independence. Each child has a book of plain pages in which the teacher can write the words he or she cannot spell. These are simple at first, but the child soon sees a purpose in organizing them and eventually in the use of alphabetical order. It is at this point, for most children, that the alphabet makes sense and the letters can be memorized in traditional order. In time the child learns how to use printed dictionaries, and there are on the market many well-illustrated dictionaries suitable for use by beginners.

Reading aloud what they have written help children to see the purpose of periods, capital letters and commas. The teacher can point out, from a familiar story printed in a book, how to indicate dialogue. When a child's book is given a place of honour alongside printed books on the library shelves, it becomes obvious to her that it must be written in a socially acceptable form. The writing of good English is common sense and is not acquired by practising English exercises but by making good use of the language.

Spontaneous writing takes a variety of forms, and develops as part of a whole situation or as a link in a chain of activities. A few examples will indicate some of the ways in which writing arose as a natural outcome of what a child was doing.

Children in one reception class used the playhouse as the basis of their science fiction play. They reproduced robot activities with great exactitude and later decided to draw them out on paper, but found the robots difficult to draw to their liking and asked their teacher to help them out. As the teacher had never watched this particular program on television she was not able to do this, but promised to try if they would tell her exactly what to draw. The children soon realized the part played by careful observation and accurate description. Later the teacher helped them to add appropriate captions beneath their pictures: "I am an alien...They must be exterminated..."

Graham, aged six, was interested in sound. The fact that his father wore a hearing aid may have been partly responsible for this. He spent a lot of time in the "sound corner", experimenting with rubber bands, a tin and string telephone, and a tuning fork. He recorded his discoveries in a book, which he took home to show his father. His words were supplemented by pictures, and at one point his teacher gave him the right word to crystallize his ideas.

"When we pluck (the rubber bands) it makes a buzzing noise. The little rubber band makes the loest noise...The longer we stretched the rubber band the hiyer the noise...We have just made a telephone. When the string was allowed to hang slack we could hear faintly. When the string was stretched tightly we could hear better...When we struck the tuning fork it made a buzzing sound...When I struck the tuning fork and tucht it it tickled me...The buzzing I heard is called vibration and vibration makes sound...The sound is cuzed by eeletrick carunt...When I put my hand on my throat I can feel it vibrate that is what makes my voice."

Graham then collected "Sounds I like to hear" and "Sounds I do not like."

Alex, aged seven, was fascinated by a set of large, solid, wooden, geometric shapes. The smooth perfection of the sphere she found particularly satisfying, and she went round the school finding "spheres". Her understanding was such that she was able to use her facts imaginatively, writing a fairy story incorporating marbles, planets and toffee apples. Pradip drew a picture of the way he came to school. He was shown a map of the district, and he drew a plan of the streets near the school. He then started to make a map book which contained the following entries:

"This is a map. It has a canal, a railway and three main roads."

"A map with a funny shape of roads."

"A map of the estate where the visitor (to the school) lived."

"The way to town."
"The way to grandma's."
"Where grandma lives."

Collections of words which sound lovely led to the writing of poetry:
"Starlight;
Candle-light;
Little Jesus Lord of Light."
"God's star is full of light,
Thank you for stars at night,
Stars that shine so bright."

"Blue sky, blue sky,
White clouds, white clouds.
All of those are very high,
But none are higher than the sky."

Children also composed their own prayers for school service: "Dear God help me to be good and always kind to ather pepol and when I grow up help me to be kind to my children. I have always wonted a little baby but I cannot have one becus I am too young."

"Dear God I am thanking you for sending baby Jesus to Mary because on Christmas day it is Jesus birthday and I hope Mary is glad when it is Jesus birthday and God sent baby Jesus to Mary and Mary said thankyou to God and now we are saying thankyou to you."

By the time they are seven many children are writing stories of considerable length. Imitating their long story books some children in one school wrote "novels", arranged in chapters, built round a plot or a character and employing the accurate use of dialogue. "The Adventures of Timothy and Tim on a Bicycle" and "The Odd-Job Man" were the titles of two of these.

When we set so-called English exercises or composition, we underestimate children's ability, we are crippling their imagination. If teachers are to liberate in children the power to communicate imaginatively what they think and feel, our first job is to inspire in them a sense of the beauty and majesty of words.

19

Helping the child to become literate

Modern society seems obsessed by the desire for premature development. Any project which promises earlier performance gets a hearing. Many parents and teachers sincerely believe that if they force a child into doing at five what they would grow into at six, then the child benefits, and they are seen to be more efficient as educators. All that we know now about the significance of maturation has little effect on this belief when it comes to the teaching of reading. Inability to recognize printed words at an early age is regarded as proof of the failure of the educational system. We rarely hear criticism against the school in which children's reading skill is precocious and ahead of their understanding.

As adults who inherit a literate environment we want our children to acquire skill in reading as soon as possible so that they can benefit from their heritage. This is right and we must do everything we can to encourage children's literary development, but we want them to develop fully and not merely seem to develop.

Some children develop quickly and are capable of reading long before they come into school. The frequently held concept of reading readiness occurring at six and a half needs to be exploded. A child may be three and a half chronologically or he may be eight, and the fact that he reaches the stage early or late is not always dependent on his intellectual capacity. This particular ability can ripen at stages which vary considerably between individual children.

In recent years people genuinely concerned with helping children to become literate have promoted schemes which claim to reduce the problem of word recognition and enable the child to read earlier. We will consider the more popular of these schemes. We will also consider more generally ways in which we can encourage literacy in our children.

Glenn Doman was a member of a team of American doctors and educators working to help children who suffered from brain injuries. They realized that children, even those suffering from brain damage, could be trained at a very early age to recognize printed words, provided the print was large enough. Glenn Doman then turned his attention to normal children and brought out a book entitled *Teach Your Baby to Read*, in which he provides parents with step-by-step instructions for training children to articulate printed words from the age of two or even younger.

Parts of Glenn Doman's argument are very soundly based. He views reading as a brain function and not as a subject to be taught in school. "Reading language", he says, "is a brain function exactly as learning language is a brain function", and again: "Everybody plus the child's environment teaches a child to understand spoken language," and likewise, he argues, to read. We could agree also with his statement that "all children want to absorb information about everything around them, and under the proper circumstances reading is one of these things". He emphasizes the importance of adult attitude and urges parents to keep reading a joyous experience, avoiding anxiety at all costs.

Unfortunately, there are major flaws in Glenn Doman's theory and the most important of these is his misinterpretation of the term reading. All those who live close to young children know that they recognize words such as "Esso", "McDonalds", "Woolworths", and that they can be helped in their powers of recognition by being told what these signs stand for. But children do this as part of an activity such as filling up at the gas station, going out to eat and so on, and we must not assume that to isolate the symbols from the activity and then to train children to say them on sight is the same thing as meeting the word naturally in the live situation.

Glenn Doman says that "very young children can read, *provided* that, in the beginning, you make the print very big". This could be a very misleading statement, for there is far, far more to the skill of reading than the remark implies.

The method of instruction prescribed by Glenn Doman seems to be based entirely on stimulus-response learning theory. Children are trained to make the correct verbal response and then are profusely rewarded when they do so correctly. We could train pigeons and rats in this way, although their responses would take the form of action rather than speech. Likewise, children of eighteen months to three years can be conditioned to respond. We can train them at this stage in their mental development to make the correct response each time we show them a word pattern. They will make the right noise, but it may mean little or nothing to them. As their thought-processes become more firmly structured they require more meaning in their learning and will lose interest in these elementary forms of response. Again, do we really want the six-year-old to "enjoy the material which would normally be presented to him when he is between eight and fourteen years of age"?

Perhaps the most distressing flaw in Glenn Doman's theory is the view he takes of the child's mind. He likens the newborn baby to an empty electronic computer and talks about placing information in a child's brain. He uses the terms information and knowledge as though they were identical. We agree entirely that the child is insatiably curious and that his thirst for knowledge is boundless. But the child's knowledge is based initially on first-hand experience. Information from other sources such as books can be grafted on to what children have discovered for themselves. To say that "children should learn to read and thus gain access to all knowledge" is equivalent to saying that children will know because they are told. But, and especially at this age, a book can offer only an extension of actual experience.

Glenn Doman also assumes that homes and parents deprive children of learning opportunities, that the child is kept all the time in the play-pen, and that schools are arid of experience. He seems to have a poor concept of what goes on in good homes and lively schools. He promises to the parent who instructs her two-year-old to recognize words a child who will spend most of the time absorbed in books. Do we want children to live second-hand in a world of books before they have lived first-hand with soil and water and sun-warmed wind? Children given good chances, will learn to recognize words as part of their environment. They will use them in due course to supplement their immediate experiences and as substitutes for them, but what they read needs the foundation of meaning, which can only be laid through adequate first-hand living during the early stages of life. There is much more to reading than recognizing and articulating words which are big enough for the child to see.

Promoters of i.t.a., the initial teaching alphabet, feel that the inconsistencies of English spelling may be a major cause of failure to read, because the conventional alphabet produces books which contain confusing variants for the child to grasp. An augmented alphabet was devised by Sir James Pitman with a view to making all words phonetic. This is not a method of teaching reading, it is a medium or alphabet. The augmented alphabet consists of forty-three letters, and each letter matches a sound. The letter "a" in the conventional alphabet stands for several sounds as in "at", "any", "want", "all", "say", "bath", and so forth. We need a different letter for each of these sounds.

Basically this is a good idea, and if i.t.a. were completely adopted our language would become phonic and more easily communicable to other nationalities. In order to use it as a teaching medium, however, we must translate printed material into i.t.a. This means that the child's learning to read is limited to material which is printed in this special way and words in the child's natural environment are ignored.

It means also that formal instruction is inevitable. What we do is ask children to ignore all printed words they find in everyday life and direct their attention to those prepared in i.t.a. The encyclopaedia at home, Grandmother's bible, Auntie's letter, and the text on John's cough-syrup are no longer available as reading material. Children must be trained to recognize word patterns they must later unlearn, and this is educationally most undesirable.

Again, the incentive of earlier reading is offered by the promoters of i.t.a. Children can be trained through phonetic drill to articulate words in print irrespective of whether those words mean anything to them. If a word pattern stimulates no corresponding idea in the child's mind, the fact that he or she can say that word can scarcely be called reading. The ability to read and write words ahead of experience has no merit at all.

A schools organizer visited a school in which i.t.a. was exclusively used in the approach to reading. She was introduced to a child of five and a half who she was told could read anything, "even the daily newspaper fresh from the press". The child was given an unopened copy of the *Daily Mirror*. He certainly could read it. In fact he "read" straight across the top of all four columns!

Too often we are told of the child's *performance*. Even educational psychologists speak of how the child *performs*, as though reading were some kind of feat which a child should be trained to do. Dr. Joyce Morris goes as far as to suggest that primary school children should be trained to read "at least mechanically". Can we wonder that children grow to mistrust

97

the printed word?

While the alphabet in general use in our country remains irregular, material printed will frequently remain non-phonetic, and phonic media such as i.t.a, which produces phonic material, will involve us in mechanical methods of teaching because they isolate children's material from their everyday life. What happens where the majority of children are concerned is that they learn the material presented by the teacher alongside material presented by the general environment. Fortunately children defeat attempts made by adults to deprive them of their right to learn from the best in word usage. Unless we lock away all traditional literature, write and read our letters in secret, veil all interesting advertisements and switch off the television, we cannot stop them learning from the alphabet they have inherited. Major reform in the alphabet should be approached at adult level; the conflict between traditional and revised usage should not be inflicted on the child.

Dr. Gattegno's reading scheme "Words in Colour" has something in common with i.t.a. in that it sets out to make English phonetically regular by using colour with letter shapes to distinguish the various sounds from which words are built. A teacher operating this scheme introduces sounds in isolation and the normal stimulus of books is deliberately ruled out. The material is not even illustrated. No attempt is made to teach reading through interest and meaning, and the learning situation is completely formal. The child is limited to the phonetic material prescribed by the scheme and rote learning is practised throughout. The advantage of the scheme is that it provides children with a complete tool, for, if they know the sounds, they can decipher any word, whether it means anything to them or not.

In recent years attempts have been made to teach reading by programed instruction. Material is prepared and presented in much the same way as the step-by-step procedure outlined by Glenn Doman. Programed instruction is, in fact, an extension of textbook instruction. The unique quality of programed learning lies in its mechanical and impersonal nature.

The idea of a reading program is that the child works individually, through small simple steps, towards the recognition of words singly and in groups. Children can work at their own pace, independent of the teacher, and they are guaranteed success. They do not suffer from competition and feelings of failure.

A few children, for reasons beyond their control, find human relationship difficult and perhaps a barrier to learning. Such children could benefit from an impersonal approach such as programed instruction gives. For the large majority of our children, learning to read is essentially an aspect of a child's relationship with adults or sometimes with especially gifted children. Providing their mistakes are not too numerous and failure is not too severe, occasional lack of success adds zest and challenge to the exploration of the printed word. To share this adventure with someone the child loves brings joy to the experience and helps to develop healthy attitudes towards literature in later life.

Some teachers develop ideas of their own and devise apparatus, work-books and games as a reading scheme in itself or as an aid to an existing scheme. Games which centre mainly around the idea of word recognition from flash cards may help a child to form a mental image of a word pattern. Generally speaking, material of this kind tests rather than teaches, and it concentrates on visual acuity.

There are logical arguments to support all these approaches to reading. In each there is much that is commendable and teachers and parents will give them careful consideration. Educators of young children are in a position to evaluate the many suggestions made to them. It is they who will decide what is of value in helping children, what they will use, and how they will use it. At all costs they must resist the pressure of promoters, however sincere, and often of public opinion. Logical arguments readily persuade adults, but the logic of children does not run along adult lines.

Sometimes interesting schemes and attractively produced material enthuse teachers. Their enthusiasm is conveyed to the children they teach and the response of these children is gratifying. Where learning to read is concerned, as with most learning, the person who helps matters far more than the methods and material she uses. Either directly or indirectly the child must learn his language from adults. How they feel about those adults and how they treat them make the difference between effective learning and failure.

Some children can and will learn to read long before they come into school. If they can learn at the age of three and enjoy reading as part of their exploration of life around them, then we should help them. We should not, however, consider these children necessarily more favoured than the child who reads later. We should avoid that glow of pride for the child who reads at four and the inclination to extend only tepid praise for the skill of a five-year-old brother in making a picture or in swimming.

The most encouraging thing we can do about helping children to become literate is to make sure they meet and enjoy good literature. Stories are perhaps the greatest means of communication between people. They provided us with our first literature and they play the leading part in our introduction of literature to the child. We tell children stories we enjoy and so convey our delight in them. We select our stories with great care and treat them as part of the child's social development.

A good story for children should be exciting and keep the child wondering what happens next. It should develop through characters the child would like to live with. It should be authentic in detail and atmosphere, packed with action and dramatic situation. It should have humour. Above all it should be well written, using words which please the child and extend her or his vocabulary, and with an opening which makes the listener sit up and take notice.

The story-teller's equipment consists of a voice children can listen to and personal interest which enables them to set the atmosphere before the story is told. As the story is re-created between teller and audience the children should become part of the story, so that they extend their own experience and learn more about themselves as they enter into it.

The story is of intrinsic value, and telling stories primarily for the moral they are intended to convey can be a misuse of this mode of communication.

While only the best is good enough for children, this does not exclude the teacher's own creative efforts. Teachers who, knowing their children well, can create their own story and let children share in creating one to their own taste and mood have an excellent means of helping children to understand the uses of their own language. These stories can take their place amongst the stories of good writers and, from time to time, the stories of great writers. Folk stories, legends, ballads and parables are all immortalized because they contain an authentic core. Their vigour vitalizes literature. Children need bedtime tales, but if they are to develop good taste in literature they must be given every chance to experience the work of recognized masters, particularly during the introductory years.

20

Problems associated with the teaching of reading

We have considered reading as part of children's heritage and as a development of speech. We have seen how the majority of our children, in spite of the various ways adults go about the teaching of reading, grow gradually and naturally into the use of words on paper. Some gain skill sooner than others, but we hope most children will make a start by the time they are seven and will be reasonably confident by the age of nine. Our educational system is designed around this assumption.

Very few children are incapable of learning to read, but each child has his or her own pace and a large percentage of our children experience considerable difficulty in learning to recognize printed words until they are about eight or nine. Most children need sympathetic help during the first two years in their junior grades; some need help all the way.

Many children on leaving the primary grades are able to recognize quite a wide range of word patterns and attach meaning to printed words when they see them. Even so, these more able children have not completed the process. Learning to read doesn't happen at one particular time. It is a continuous experience with its roots in the child's first days, or even hours, of life, and we continue throughout life to acquire further skill in it.

Sometimes the teacher of a less able eight-year-old child blames primary teachers for not having done their job. This attitude is not likely to help and children may feel they have committed a crime. They are often very anxious to read and are every bit as frustrated as the teacher when they fail to make any progress.

The term "problem" associated with the teaching of reading is used to denote inability on the part of the child to acquire the skill of recognizing words in print. We shall in this chapter consider the causes which delay development of the skill. We shall also consider precocious performance, for many of us have witnessed the detrimental effects of premature reading skill on the child.

It is at the secondary school stages that we can assess the incidence of non-readers. One enquiry in the West Riding found 1.73 per cent of secondary age children in this class. Of these, 0.99 were boys and 0.74 were girls. Children experienced difficulty for one or more of the following reasons: mental problems, illness and absence from school, speech defects, poor home environment and nervousness. The possibilities of faulty teaching and poor facilities in school were not mentioned.

These figures suggest that in spite of extra help given to those children who find reading a problem, not all of our children acquire the skill during their school education. During the Second World War reading classes for men in the Forces were highly popular and successful. These were men motivated by their need to communicate with home. They proved that they could learn to read. Why didn't they do so in school?

A consideration of the difficulties which faced some individual children may help to elucidate the nature of the problems which hinder non-readers.

At the age of four, Eric developed a hip problem. He spent the next twelve years in hospital and for much of that time he had to lie on his back with his leg suspended in a frame. Occasionally he was allowed to go home for a few days, but his parents were poor and he was rarely taken anywhere exciting. In his condition even the hospital school could do very little and he reached the age of fifteen unable to read or write. The local authority then provided two hours per week individual tuition, in the hope that Eric would be equipped to cope when he was ready to leave the hospital and take his place in society.

His teacher realized from the start that easy reading material of the commercially produced type was useless. Not only was the content childish, it referred to experiences he had never had. Even simple words such as "lake", "race", "market", or "boat" conjured a weak image in Eric's mind or none at all. The only words which meant much to him were "ceiling", "nurse", "bed", "sheets", "injections", and so on, and his teacher made him books using these words and such ideas as he might meet on radio programs, which were his only contact with the world.

As the first excitement of the teacher's visits wore off, Eric's efforts diminished. He had few responsibilities, his life was ordered for him, he had no ambition apart from leaving the hospital and living at home. His release brought disillusionment. Neighbouring children tormented him about his braces. The teacher tried to continue his lessons by inviting him to her home or by visiting him in his. Again children teased him about learning to read at sixteen. Eric gradually lost even the shreds of desire to make the effort. He could recognize the right bus, pay his fare, and spend the meagre money he earned at the clerical job he'd been found. What else mattered?

The odds against Eric becoming a skilful reader were great. He was not intellectually strong to begin with and his unfortunate circumstances and limited environment did nothing to promote his intellectual development. He had few words with which to read because few words had been given him, and those he had lacked the meaning which results from experience. Attempts to help him overcome his difficulties came too late. Most important of all, he lacked incentive; there was no inner power to drive him into using his limited resources effectively. Eric's aspirations were so low that learning to read seemed purposeless.

At the best of times Timothy's hearing was not good. When he had a cold he was practically deaf. At the age of seven he had made little progress with reading and had begun to stutter. Timothy was quite intelligent, but lack of success in his work made him feel less able than others and he had little confidence in himself. He was provided with a hearing aid, and an understanding teacher gave him small jobs which made him feel important and responsible. He became a person who counted in the classroom and this gave him confidence. His stutter disappeared and his reading began to develop.

Silva was a disruptive element in the school from the start. Her home background was a very disturbed one, with mother admitted to a mental hospital at varying intervals. Silva often wandered from home and when she returned she was beaten by her father. What she most needed was a calm, stable atmosphere, yet she destroyed every attempt on the part of her teacher to provide it. She was not unintelligent, but her speech was poor and she was unable to concentrate for more than a few minutes at a time. If she was left alone with a book she would tear it up.

Silva arrived in school one morning with terrible welts on her back and thighs. The teacher informed the authorities. They investigated and Silva was eventually placed in another home. She showed signs of responding to the patient care of the people in charge of her and she became more amenable in school. She made a number of scrap-books and started to paint, but there was still much she needed before she could be helped to recognize printed words. She left the primary grades virtually a non-starter.

Brian was a very different problem. He came from a professional home and his parents had him reading to visitors by the age of four. Before entering school he could "read" any daily newspaper, information printed on signs, even the notices in restaurants. When asked a question, however, he would stutter or fall silent.

On his first day in school Brian made for the wood-working bench. He refused to go near the book corner or to make any books; the word "book" alone evoked an emotional reaction. He spent most of his time working with his hands and adding forbidden words to his vocabulary. His teacher began to worry about his attitude to books and reading, wondering whether he had turned against them for life.

One day a child brought a rabbit to school and asked Brian to help him make a hutch for it. Brian's skill in woodwork enabled the two boys to produce a very creditable home for the rabbit. The teacher seized the opportunity. "Other people would like to make a fine hutch like yours", she encouraged him. "Could you put some instructions into this big scrapbook in my room?"

Brian consented, but his instructions took the form of pictures. "You draw well," the teacher told him, "but the pictures don't tell anyone by themselves how to make the hutch. You must explain them." Brian added suitable notes to the pictures. This was his first book work since he entered school. Gradually he discovered a new delight in books and the joy of reading was opened to him.

From these examples we could define a number of reasons for reading disability. Physical causes are perhaps the most obvious. Vision, hearing or speech problems mean that the child is not physically equipped to read. Poor general health and poor nutrition mean that she or he lacks the vitality required to tackle a difficult job. Illness and absence from school deprive the child of the chance of a good reading environment, unless the home is well endowed. An intelligent child in a literate home, on the other hand, may develop the skill when she is ill because there are fewer alternative interests when she is confined to bed.

Children with poor home backgrounds are handicapped in a number of ways. Their experiences and consequently their vocabulary are restricted, their attitude to books is undeveloped, they lack the support of parents, who may be apathetic or indifferent, like the mother who refused to let her child wear glasses in order to avoid the responsibility of looking after them.

Less obvious and more difficult to remedy are psychological causes. Anxiety, emotional disturbance, negative emotional attitudes such as resentment, apathy or inferior feelings, and Brian's urge to resist parental pressure all take time to develop and time to break down.

Much always depends on the provision made by the school, and most important of all is the attitude of the teacher and the approach used. It is from these same factors that remedies for the child's disability can be found.

Anxiety is perhaps the greatest handicap to a child where reading is concerned and anxiety on the part of the child is generally caused by the anxiety of parents or teacher. Nowadays parental anxiety tends to increase. It may be that parents feel guilty because television in the home means that they do less reading. In spite of its popularity television has not yet been accepted as a completely desirable medium in society. Why is reading approved of and television disapproved of? Parents watch television, but compensate by putting extra pressure on their children to achieve literacy.

Teachers are sensitive to this pressure on the part of parents. Many share the parents' mistakenly logical view and firmly believe that the sooner the child articulates words the more likely she or he is to become academically sound. Skill in reading is a status symbol and must be achieved no matter what the costs are to the child. We have still many parents and teachers, even principals and consultants who assess the success of a school on the facility with which a child reads aloud the printed word.

Much of this anxiety is due to the unfortunate effects of being unable to read in modern society. In our existing system of education the slow readers in the junior grades get left behind. As the gap widens between their achievement and that of their friends, they lose confidence and their attitude to their work deteriorates. Eventually they lose the desire to try. The more intelligent the child is, the more sensitive she or he is to failure, and this intelligence may go unrecognized by selective procedure when crucial selective tests are given.

Anxiety on the part of parent or teacher may prevent

them from recognizing the true cause of failure. For instance, a child who appears slow to learn may just be late, rather than slow, to learn. Jason was a quiet, dreamy child. He was readily absorbed in watching a bee plunder a flower for honey or a bricklayer shaping the corner of a wall. He would spend hours dismantling a clock or fashioning a boat from balsawood. He loved to listen to stories or poetry, and would enjoy turning the pages of a book but writing or reading words on paper had little appeal until he was nearly eight. By the age of nine he was devoted to books and was quickly caught up in the magic of their contents. We would have spoilt reading for Jason if we had tried to hurry him.

Sometimes a child suffers from dyslexia. He may be intelligent, come from a good home, show no sign of emotional disturbance, physical disability or brain-damage, and yet be quite unable to recognize word patterns. A dyslexic child cannot remember the shape of words. If they try to write a word the letters appear in the wrong order, or they may write the word backwards.

The causes of dyslexia are not fully understood, but a number of eminent personalities have been afflicted. Keats found spelling and reading a problem. Picasso never mastered the sequence of the alphabet. Hans Andersen was believed to be dyslexic. There are about 75 000 dyslexic children of school age in England. Most of them are boys, and a centre for treatment has been established in Gray's Inn Road, London, under the direction of Dr. Bannatyre. Here, interest in reading is awakened by methods similar to those described in this book. Dyslexic children must be given help before they are nine, otherwise they cannot benefit from school education.

Such children are frequently misunderstood. Parents who know their children are intelligent are disappointed by their failure to read, and this disappointment is quickly conveyed to the children, who feel that they have let their parents down. A teacher may think an intelligent dyslexic is lazy or defiant or ridiculing her. If they are capable, why do they remain indifferent to the teacher's attention? The child's problem is increased when such a situation develops.

What happens to the children who fail to make the grade? Often they are signaled out and given extra doses of the medicine which has already failed. The practice of reading is isolated from other activities and word recognition becomes a drill, distasteful in spite of efforts to ginger it up.

Children rarely benefit from being treated apart from

the group. It is distressing to find teachers who seem to think that their main contribution in the school is to hear slow readers stumble over printed words. The child may appreciate the kindly attempts to help, but the image retained of such a teacher in later years is scarcely that of an inspired teacher.

The gifted reader may also need sympathy and special help. It is tempting for parents to exploit a young child's intellect. The prodigy is a credit to parents and it takes a very unselfish parent to resist showing off feats to their friends. Intelligent children are easy to teach, anxious to please, and sensitive to what is required of them. They acquire words quickly and, because they are intelligent, may grasp the meaning of a word at second hand from an adult before experience has had time to prepare the ground. The words they are encouraged to say and read may have insecure conceptual foundations. Reading then becomes a circus act performed before an approving audience.

Joanna was able to read fluently when she entered school. Already books dominated her life. She would rather read about soil than play with it. She lived more in the world of print than in the real world and was impatient with children who didn't understand what she said to them. She knew less about other children than was known by an unintelligent child from a disadvantaged home. She preferred the safe world of her books to the hazards and adventure of making friends. She had to be weaned away from her books and encouraged to play. Eventually "dressing-up" caught her imaginative interest and it was through spontaneous dramatic play that she learned to communicate with others and so learned to enjoy a measure of normal childhood. Even so, her parents felt she was wasting her time and looked for the day when she could get into the junior grades and "do something worthwhile."

Problems associated with the teaching of reading stem from many aspects of the child's total personal pattern. We cannot consider them in isolation. The more deeply we consider them, the more aware we become of the integrated nature of the child's learning. Learning to read is an inseparable part of the child's whole development. It depends as much on the stage a child has reached in his or her awareness of the surrounding world as it does on the material and help we provide. The successful acquisition of the skill depends on the harmonious relationship between physical and psychological systems.

Children in our society grow up in a world of words.

Those words come to have meaning because they are part of their living. Problems begin to arise when we try to isolate printed words and treat them as things apart instead of treating them as one aspect of communication. Much of what takes place in some schools is little more than practising the skill of word recognition. When the learning is active and vital very little time need be spent on word analysis and practising. "Hearing children read" as a regular drill may assure the teacher that the child can recognize word patterns, but it does little to further reading skill. The *use* the child can make of word in print is much more a measure of comprehension than mere articulation can ever be.

The argument that children like someone to hear them read is often quoted in support of the practice. Children will do much to secure the approval of adults and direct their precious attention towards themselves. Children know that they are assured of attention if they wave a reader in front of the teacher, principal, consultant, or other visitor to the school. They know that few adults will resist this approach. Their sense of achievement should not depend on completing one book after another. Joy in the content of books is the real reward of a skill mastered. Adult attitudes which foster these modes of behaviour in children do not help solve problems but rather help make them.

When Trevor came into school at the age of five, he had not started to read in spite of attempts made at home to help him. He was an intelligent boy, well aware of the anxiety of his parents. He saw a number of children reading and obviously enjoying the books in the classroom. Trevor settled down with a book and with one eye on his teacher simulated the skill of the older children. He made sure that his teacher "saw him reading" several times a day, but if another child came to share his book he shut it up and put it away. It was some weeks before his teacher was able to free Trevor sufficiently from parental anxiety and enable him to get absorbed in picture-making and painting and in the exploration of materials which would lay the foundation of his later reading skill.

Young children are very dependent on adults, particularly on those they love. The attitude of parents and teachers to anything they do is of supreme importance. Where the teaching of reading is concerned the right relationship between child and adult is far more influential than the approach, the methods, or the material used.

Conclusion: parents and teachers

The education of children is the joint responsibility of parents and teachers. In the development of language the essential nature of this partnership is clearly perceived. Children are favoured when they share language with parents and teachers who are alive to the joy of their mother tongue and who are sensitive to the vital spirit of language in all its diversified forms. Children will learn to love and enjoy English because those who teach them love and enjoy it.

Parents are directly responsible for providing their children with the essential tool of their learning, and if children's homes have failed to equip them well verbally they face school with a handicap which may very well cripple them personally as well as intellectually. Teachers have few illusions about the help they can give. Verbal foundations must be well laid during the early stages of development, and even the most articulate and imaginative teacher finds great difficulty in developing the child's linguistic skills when those foundations are weak.

In our society we do not leave the task of raising children to parents alone. Nor do we believe in a system which delegates this essential responsibility to the state alone. The whole of our educational procedure is based on our belief in a balance of responsibility between parents and teachers. Before we ever plan for the child within the system we should do well to consider the true nature of this partnership. The Plowden Committee were clear-minded about this and made it an important issue in their Report:

"One of the essentials for educational advance is a closer partnership between the two parties to every child's education....Homes and schools interact continuously" (102). "It has long been recognized that education is concerned with the whole person: henceforth it must be concerned with the whole family" (129).

Children learn more about language in the four or five years before entering school than they will ever learn again within the same span of time. What they learn about language in all its diversity must be grafted during their school years on to the language they already have. It is no good expecting children to learn about reading or writing, about speaking or thinking, at any particular stage in their lives. Parents must prepare the ground and support the growing skill in the child. Teachers must recognize the contribution of parents and show a perpetual willingness to acquaint them with what they try to do in school. Such attitudes of co-operation, will indirectly reinforce all children learn as their linguistic confidence grows.

Suggestions For Further Reading

Allport, Gordon W. *Pattern and Growth of Personality*. New York and London: Holt, Rinehart and Winston, 1961.

Almy, Millie. "A Child's Right to Play." *Childhood Education* 60 (1984):350

Archer, H., and Parry, M. *Preschool Education*. London: Schools Council Publication, Macmillan, 1975.

Archer, H., and Parry, M. *Two to Five*. London: Macmillan Educational, 1975.

Arnold, H.; Johnson, S.; and Southgate, V. *Extending Beginning Reading*. London: Heinemann Educational Books/Schools Council, 1981.

Bate, M.; Cleave, S.; and Jowett, S. *And So To School*. Windsor: NFER-Nelson, 1982.

Battle, S.; Clift, P. S.; and Cyster, R. *Parental Involvement in Primary Schools*. Slough: NFER, 1980.

Bennett, J. *Reaching Out*. Stroud, Gloucester: Thimble Press, 1983.

Bereiter C., and Englemann, S. *Teaching Disadvantaged Children in the Pre-School*. Englewood Cliffs, NJ: Prentice-Hall, 1966.

Bernstein, B. *A Brief Account of the Theory of Codes in Social Relationships and Language*. London: Routledge & Kegan Paul, 1973.

Blackstone, T., and Mortinmore, J. *Disadvantage and Education*. London: Heinemann, 1982.

Board of Education for the City of North York. *Look! Hear!* 1983.

Boyers, P.; Brereton, A.; and Redman, S. *An Approach to Primary Science*. London: Macmillan Educational, 1969.

Brennan, W. K. *Shaping the Education of Slow Learners*. London: Routledge & Kegan Paul, 1974.

Britton, J. *Language and Learning*. Harmondsworth: Penguin, 1970.

Brown, G.; Modgil, C.; and Modgil, S., eds. *Jean Piaget: An Interdisciplinary Critique*. London: Routledge & Kegan Paul, 1983.

Bruner, J. "The ontogenesis of speech acts." *Journal of Child Language* 2:1-19.

Bruner, J. S. *Under Five in Britain*. London: Grant McIntyre, 1980.

Bruner, J. S.; Jolly, A.; and Sylva, K., eds. *Play: Its Role in Development and Evolution.* Harmondsworth: Penguin, 1976.

Bryant, P. *Perception and Understanding in Young Children: an Experimental Approach.* London: Methuen, 1974.

Burchell, B.; Mortimore, J; and Tizard, B. *Involving Parents in Nursery and Infant Schools: A Source Book for Teachers.* London: Grant McIntyre, 1981.

Butterworth, G., ed. *Infancy and Epistemology: an Evaluation of Piaget's Theory.* Brighton: Harvester Press, 1981.

Cashdan, A., and Grugeon, E., eds. *Language in Education.* London: Routledge & Kegan Paul/Open University, 1972.

Cass, J. E. *The Significance of Children's Play.* London: Batsford, 1971.

Chazan, Maurice, and Laing, Alice F. *Children with Special Needs: The Early Years.* Milton Keynes: Open University Press, 1982.

Cherry, Clare. *Creative Play for the Developing Child.* Belmont, CA: Fearon-Petman Publishers Inc., 1976.

Chomsky, C.S. *The Acquisition of Syntax in Children from Five to Ten.* Cambridge, MA: MIT Press, 1969.

Clarke, A. D. B., and Clarke, A. M. *Practical Help for Parents of Retarded Children.* Hull: Hull Society for Mentally Handicapped Children, 1969.

Clay, Marie. *What Did I Write?* London: Heinemann Educational Books, 1975.

Conger, J. J.; Kagan, J.; and Mussen, P. H. *Child Development and Personality.* 5th ed. New York: Harper and Row, 1979.

Copeland, R. *How Children Learn Mathematics—Teaching Implications of Piaget's Research.* New York: Macmillan, 1984.

Crowe, B. *The Playgroup Movement.* London: Allen & Unwin, 1971.

Day, Barbara. *Early Childhood Education.* Toronto: Macmillan, 1983.

Department of Education and Science. *Mathematics Counts.* (The Cockcroft Report). London: HMSO, 1982.

Department of Education and Science. *Mathematics 5-11.* London: HMSO, 1979.

Donaldson, M. *Children's Minds.* London: Fontana, 1978.

Douglas, J. W. B. *The Home and the School.* A study of ability and attainment in the primary school, with an introduction by Professor D. V. Glass. London: MacGibbon and Kee, 1964.

Federation of Women Teachers' Associations of Ontario. *Active Learning in the Early School Years*. 1986.

Federation of Women Teachers' Associations of Ontario. *FWTAO Response to Herald A Child*. 1982.

Fontana, D., ed. *The Education of the Young Child*. 2nd ed. Oxford: Basil Blackwell, 1984.

Furth, H. *Thinking without Language*. Illinois: The Free Press of Glencoe, 1966.

Getzels, J. W., and Jackson, P. W. *Creativity and Intelligence*. New York: Wiley, 1962.

Gibran, Kahlil. *The Prophet*. London: Heinemann, 1956.

Ginsburg, H., and Opper, S. *Piaget's Theory of Intellectual Development*. Englewood Cliffs, NJ: Prentice-Hall Inc., 1979.

Goodman, Y.M. "Using children's reading miscues for new teaching strategies." *Reading Teacher* 23:455-459.

Gulliford, R., and Tansley, A. F. *The Education of Slow-learning Children*. London: Routledge & Kegan Paul, 1961. (Paperback 1966).

Halliday, M. *Learning How to Mean*. London: Edward Arnold, 1975.

Hohmann, Mary et al. *Young Children in Action*. Ypsilanti, MI: The High-Scope Press, 1979.

Holdaway, D. *The Foundations of Literacy*. New York: Ashton Scholastic, 1979.

Horner, P.H. *Reading: an Introduction*. London: Heinemann Educational Books, 1972.

Horowitz, Frances Degen ed. *Review of Child Development Research*. Chicago: University of Chicago Press, 1975.

Hutt, C. *Play and Learning*. New York: Gardner Press, 1979.

Illingworth, R. S. *The Normal School Child and His Problems, Physical and Emotional*. London: Heinemann, 1964.

Isenberg, Joan P., and Jacobs, Judith E. *Playthings as Learning Tools*. Toronto: John Wiley and Sons, 1982.

Jeffreys, M.V.C. *Personal Values in the Modern World*. Harmondsworth, Penguin, 1962.

Kellmer Pringle, M. *The Needs of Children*. London: Hutchinson.1974.

Kernig, W., and McKenzie, M. *The Challenge of Informal Education*. London: Darton, Longman and Todd, 1975.

Lane, S., and Kemp, M. *Approaches to Writing and Language*. London: Ward Lock, 1981.

Lewis, M.M. *Language, Thought and Personality*. London: Harrap, 1963.

Lloyd, J., and Marzollo, J. *Learning Through Play*. London: Allen & Unwin, 1974.

Lovell, K. *The Growth of Basic Scientific and Mathematical Concepts*. London: University of London Press, 1961.

Luria, A.R., and Yudovich, F.I. *Speech and the Development of Mental Processes in the Child*. Harmondsworth: Penguin, 1971.

Mackay, D. *Breakthrough to Literacy*. Harlow: Longman, 1970.

Manning, K., and Sharp, A. *Structuring Play in the Early Years at School*. London: Ward Lock Educational Schools Council, 1977.

Marshall, Sybil. *Adventure in Creative Education*. London: Pergamon, 1968.

Marshall, Sybil. *An Experiment in Education*. Cambridge: Cambridge University Press, 1963.

Marshall, Sybil. *Aspects of Artwork*. London: Evans, 1970.

Matthews, G., ed. *Mathematics Through School*. London: John Murray, 1972.

Matthews, J., ed. *Trends in Primary Education*. London: Peter Owen, 1975.

McNally, J., and Murray, W. *Key Words to Literacy and the Teaching of Reading*. London: Schoolmaster Publishing Company, 1962.

McNeill, D. *The Acquisition of Language: The Study of Developmental Linguistics*. New York: Harper and Row, 1970.

Mischel, W. *Introduction to Personality*. 3rd ed. New York: Holt, Rinehart and Winston, 1981.

Modgil, C., and Modgil, S., eds. *Jean Piaget: Consensus and Controversy*. London: Holt, Rinehart and Winston, 1982.

Modgil, C., and Modgil, S. *Piagetian Research: Compilation and Commentary*. Windsor: NFER, 1976.

Munion, C., ed. *The Baby Book*. Twickenham: Hamlyn, 1982. (Softcover ed. 1984).

Newson, E., and Newson J. *Four Years Old in an Urban Community*. London: Allen & Unwin, 1963. (Penguin ed. 1970).

Newson, E., and Newson J. *Patterns of Infant Care in an Urban Community*. London: Allen & Unwin, 1963. (Penguin ed. 1975).

Newson, E., and Newson J. *Seven Years Old in an Urban Community.* London: Allen & Unwin, 1976.

Nuffield Mathematics. *I Do and I Understand, Beginnings.* London: John Murray, 1967.

Nuffield Mathematics 5-11. *Teachers' Handbooks 1 and 2.* Harlow: Longman, 1979.

Ontario Ministry of Education. *Drama in the Formative Years.* 1984.

Ontario Ministry of Education. *Early Primary Education Project, draft document.* April,1985.

Ontario Ministry of Education. *The Formative Years; Education in the Primary and Junior Division; Complexities of Childhood Chart.* 1975.

Ontario Ministry of Education. *Shared Discovery.* 1985.

Ontario Ministry of Education and the Ministry of Colleges and Universities. "Early Primary Education." *Education Ontario Supplement.* October, 1984.

Opie, I., and Opie, P. *The Lore and Language of School Children.* London: Oxford University Press, 1959.

Painter, M.; Roy, C.; and Sylva, K. *Childwatching at Playgroup and Nursery School.* London: Grant McIntyre, 1980.

Phillips, J.L. *Piaget's Theory: a Primer.* San Francisco, W. H. Freemen & Co., 1981.

Piaget, J. *The Child's Conception of Number.* (International Library of Psychology). London: Routledge & Kegan Paul, 1952.

Piaget, J. *The Child's Conception of Physical Causality.* (International Library of Psychology). London: Routledge & Kegan Paul, 1930.

Piaget, J. *The Child's Conception of the World.* (International Library of Psychology). London: Routledge & Kegan Paul, 1929.

Piaget, J. *The Child's Construction of Reality.* (International Library of Psychology). London: Routledge & Kegan Paul, 1955.

Piaget, J. *Judgement and Reasoning in the Child.* (International Library of Psychology). London: Routledge & Kegan Paul, 1928.

Piaget, J. *The Language and Thought of the Child.* London: Routledge & Kegan Paul, 1960.

Piaget, J., and Inhelder, B. *The Growth of Logical Thinking from Childhood to Adolescence.* London: Routledge & Kegan Paul, 1958

Pluckrose, H.A. *Art.* London: Macmillan, 1972.

Pluckrose, H.A. *A Source Book of Picture Making*. London: Evans, 1978.

Pringle, M. K. *The Needs of Children*. London: Hutchinson, 1974.

Read, Sir Herbert. *Education Through Art*. London: Faber, 1958.

Roberts, V. *Playing, Learning and Living*. Oxford: Basil Blackwell, 1971.

Rosen, C., and Rosen, H. *The Language of Primary School Children*. Harmondsworth: Penguin, 1973.

Schondell, F. *Backwardness in the Basic Subjects*. Edinburgh: Oliver & Boyd, 1959.

Schools Mathematics Project. *Pointers*. Cambridge: Cambridge University Press, 1984.

Schweinhart, Lawrence, and Weikart, David. "The Promise of Early Childhood Education." *Phi Delta Kappan*. April, 1985.

Schweinhart, Lawrence, and Weikart, David. *Young Children Grow Up*. Ypsilanti, MI: The High-Scope Press, 1980.

Sheridan, M. D. *Children's Developmental Progress*. London: NFER, 1975.

Shinman, S. M. *A Chance For Every Child? Access and Response to Pre-School Provision*. London: Tavistock, 1981.

Siberman, Charles. "Crisis in the Classroom: Children and their Primary Schools." *A Report of the Central Advisory Council for Education*. England: Random House, 1970.

Smith, T. *Parents and Preschool*. London: Grant McIntyre, 1980.

Stallibrass, A. *The Self-Respecting Child*. London: Thames and Hudson, 1974.

Sylva, K. Play and Learning. In *The Biology Of Play*, eds. B. Tizard and D. Harvey. London: Heinemann, 1977.

Tanner, J. M. *Education and Physical Growth*. Madison: International University Press, Inc., 1961.

Toronto Board of Education. *Observing Children*. Toronto Board Observation Project. 1980.

Tough, J. *The Development of Meaning: A Study of Children's Use of Language*. London: Allen & Unwin, 1976.

Tough, J. *Focus on Meaning*. London: Allen & Unwin, 1974.

Tough, J. *Listening to Children Talking: A guide to the appraisal of children's use of language*. London: Ward Lock Educational, 1976.

Tough, J. *Talking and Learning: A guide to fostering communication skills in Nursery and Infant Schools*. London: Ward Lock Educational, 1977.

Vygotsky, L.S. *Thought and Language*. Cambridge, MA: MIT Press, 1934.

Webb, L. *Children With Special Needs in the Infant School*. London: Collins Fontant Books, 1967.

Weikart, D.P. "Early Primary Education Project Ontario Supplement." Ontario Ministry of Education and Ministry of Colleges and Universities. October, 1984.

Weininger, Otto. *Out of the Minds of Babes: The Strength of Children's Feelings*. Springfield, IL: Charles C. Thomas, 1982.

Weininger, Otto. *Play and Education*. Springfield, IL: Charles C. Thomas, 1979.

Wells, C.G. *Language Development in the Preschool*. Cambridge: Cambridge University Press, 1984.

Whittaker, D.E. *Mathematics Through Discovery*. Teachers' book and three volumes. London: Harrap, 1965.

White, Burton. *The First Three Years of Life*. New York: Avon Books, 1978.

Wilkinson, A. *The Foundations of Language*. London: Oxford, 1971.

Wolfendale, S. *Parental Participation in Children's Development and Education*. Special Aspects of Education. London: Gordon and Breach, 1983.

Wood, D.; McMalion, L; and Granston, Y. *Working With The Under Fives*. London: Grant McIntyre, 1980.

Yardley, A. *Preparing Your Child For School*. Parents' Guides. Danbury, CT: Franklin Watts Limited, 1980.

Index

40; stages in development of 8; teacher's 42 58-9 66-7

stories, value of 64-5 100

symbols, developing use of 34; discriminating between 35; learning to use 19-20; mathematical 36-7; personal meaning of 35-6; range of humans' 19 21; use in primary schools 21

talking, in school 17-18 62

tape-recorder, as aid to good speech 65

Teach Your Baby to Read 95

telephone, as aid to good speech 65-6

television programmes 66

thought, development of 19-20

24-5; Piaget's view of 24-5; words and 10 26-7

vocabulary, building the child's 6 11-12 37 59 88-9

words, exploration and 4; expressive use of 46; in action 61; in education 22 44; in print 50-1 59-60 68 71-2; living nature of 13; meaning of 2-4 10-12; playing with 47-8 74; pleasure of 47; recognition of 74; significance of 1 49 58; thought and 10 26-7

'Words in Colour' (Dr. Gategno's reading scheme) 98

writing, letter- 86; imaginative 87-8; materials 89-90